THINK
PLAN
& SUCCEED BIG

BY   INVOLVING   GOD

SIMPLE WAYS TO ACHIEVE UNCOMMON SUCCESS IN LIFE

Dr. JULIAN THOMAS

Terrance &
Thaia
Your gift is going to
open up new avenues
for your family
Dr Jul
Thm

ISBN 978-1-68197-492-7 (paperback)
ISBN 978-1-68197-619-8 (hardcover)
ISBN 978-1-68197-493-4 (digital)

Christian Faith Publishing, Inc.
296 Chestnut Street
Meadville, PA 16335
www.christianfaithpublishing.com

Front cover images are credited to:

Presenter Media
4416 S Technology Dr.
Sioux Falls, SD 57106 USA
Ph (605) 274-2424
http://www.presentermedia.com
Businessman Silhouette Watching
Item# 15022 Type: Presentation Clipart
Businesswoman Silhouette Folder
Item#15029 Type: Presentation Clipart

Printed in the United States of America

TESTIMONIALS

Many books talk about success, but Dr. J's book helps you build a realistic plan to achieve it. He shares such great wisdom and insight that motivates me every time I read it. I'm truly inspired by his message, and I'm sure you will be inspired as well!

Vanessa Bell Armstrong
Gospel Recording Artist,
Gospel Music Hall of Fame Inductee

I have read many books on success and leadership that have made very interesting points, but never anything that transformed my thinking into greater possibilities. We often hear terms like "thinking outside of the box". However, most times all we do is think inside of a "bigger box". Dr. Js' strategy connects us to the type of thinking and planning where no limits become our reality.

Superintendent, Dr. Terry Ellison
Senior Pastor
New life Church of God in Christ (COGIC)

Success doesn't just happen. Dr. Thomas gives you a step-by-step approach to one of life's greatest challenges. This book is full of actionable revelations that will open your mind to the greater future that awaits you. He has developed a brilliant and motivating resource that will equip you to be intentional about the plan God has for your life. Pick up a copy, take action, and experience the life of abundance you were meant to have!

Dr. Jevonnah "Lady J" Ellison
Leading Life & Business Coach
Founder of Maximum Potential Academy & The Leading Ladies Mastermind

Dr. Thomas speaks cogently and fluently as he gives major life-changing instructions that will revolutionize your way of thinking. He emphasizes that we should not settle where we are; there's more for us to discover about ourselves and God's plan for succeeding in life. God wants us to envision our success through His eyes. I've read many books on success and taught many lessons on the subject, but I have never had one like this. Every page is filled with flavoring, thought-provoking, and exhilarating insight. Now is the time for you to Think, Plan, and Succeed by involving God in your efforts! Don't just read it, meditate on it, internalize it, and apply it; then you will see and experience success in a BIG way!

Bishop, Dr. Harvey B. Bee
Senior Pastor
Christian Fellowship Church (CFC)

ACKNOWLEDGEMENTS

First and foremost I'd like to thank my Lord and Savior Jesus Christ for his saving grace. To the love of my life, my wife, Tamika, thank you for being my constant source of inspiration since the beginning of this journey. You are the best thing that has ever happened to me. I love you. To my wonderful children Sidarien, India, and Julian "Jay" Jr. remember that you can do all things through Christ who gives you strength. I love you too. To my parents Paul and Pearl, I love you, thank you for being a great example of godly parents, for covering me with prayer, and teaching me the values that have shaped my character. To my siblings Chuck, Shona, and Matthew, you have what it takes to think, plan, and succeed big in life! I love you all. To my departed Sister Tan, thank you for smiling down on me. I love and miss you. To my former and current Pastors, mentors, and friends, thank you from the bottom of my heart for the authentic love and support you've shown throughout my life. To my editor Lesley Dahl, you're the best!

CONTENTS

PREFACE

I've written this book with you in mind, especially those of you who are eager to begin exciting new chapters in your lives and ready to live more purposefully. Our Creator wired every one of us with unique gifts and unrealized ability. Whether we recognize it or not, we all have something incredibly valuable to offer, a service to provide, an idea to develop; and we owe it to ourselves and to others to expand our reach and share our gifts with the world.

I've always been an idealist, and God has given me the power and wisdom to carry situations, not because I was deserving or special, but because he has a plan for my life. That plan has literally taken me on a journey around the world and caused me to experience uncommon success both personally and professionally from advising battle-weary leaders in the mangled ruins of Saddam Hussein's compounds, to having courtly evening dinners with senior Japanese officials. With the deepest sense of humility, I'm grateful to have served causes that were greater than I. I believe that God also has big plans for you. You might be at a cross-roads and feel stuck, lost, and need clarity like I needed, but today you can embark on an amazing journey of self-discovery and transformation that will put you on the best path toward success. Whether it's becoming an entrepreneur, launching a non-profit organization, negotiating business deals, serving in ministry, or simply trying to build better relationships, etc., you have the potential to think, develop a plan, and succeed big!

INTRODUCTION

FOR BEST RESULTS, APPLY THESE CONCEPTS TO YOUR LIFE

Countless books, blogs, and articles have been written about success in terms of theory. My goal is to connect with you on a visceral level and show you how to experience success in reality. Over the past twenty years, I have come across strategies, techniques, and procedures to help thousands of people around the globe enjoy more promising lives. While this book was written by one author, it is a combination of ideas and thoughts from very insightful people who've selflessly shared their knowledge within the public domain. Casually reading through this book can inspire you and put you on the path to experiencing both personal and professional success, however, for best results you must go beyond reading it and apply the hard-won wisdom that I share to experience uncommon success in life!

BIG is an acronym I created that simply means "by involving God." This means we must make God the greatest factor in our planning efforts and the most important priority in all our undertakings. I believe we can do great things with our lives and succeed *big*. With regard to spiritual issues, it is second nature to put God first; but in other areas of our lives, there are times when we forget to consult him. It is easy to think if we work hard enough and strategize well enough then we will succeed on our own. In some cases this may be true, but the benefit of involving God in all our endeavors is that we get to establish a deeper connection, confidence, and dependence on him. I believe this is the real purpose of life. Besides, if we can accomplish our dreams through our own abilities and resources then our dreams are too small. To do big things, you'll need a big God and just a little bit of faith. Faith is one of the most powerful forces governing this earth. If you learn to engage your faith and apply the practical strategies throughout this book, you can live with more clarity, precision, and effectiveness. If you've ever wrestled with procrastination or small thinking, this book is for you. If you're unsure of how to accomplish your goals, this book will show you how. Regardless of your present age, social status, or condition, if you apply the strategic principles in this book, you will be on the right path to experience maximum fulfillment and achieve God's will for your life.

You will find some chapters that are diagnostic and other sections anecdotal because they stem from my personal stories and experiences. At some point we must come to the conclusion that our success hinges on what we learn, what we do, what we have done, and what we have not done. Our experiences serve as rectors in the university of our lives and help shape who we are. They teach us what we do not know about ourselves. What we learn from our experiences should prompt us to take inventory of what is wrong in our lives and take steps toward making it right. My mother always said, "When you know better, you should do better." Today you've taken a good step toward becoming a better version of yourself by reading this book.

PUSH (persist until success happens) is another acronym I use to drive people beyond their sticking points. It simply means never give up, stick with it! Whatever *it* is for you. Successful people are relentlessly determined to continue steadfastly in their courses of action, making adjustments where necessary to get the best results.

Even when challenges become stressful or complicated, they know that quitting is not an option. They maintain a can-do attitude and tenacious approach toward accomplishing their goals. They fight the good fight of faith and are persistent in looking for new solutions and strategies when previous plans have failed.

At the end of each section I've included a PUSH page. Be sure to use the Life Application Exercises on the PUSH page to help build strategic plans for your life. Also, you may use the PUSH pages to take notes, journal your thoughts, and draft blueprints for your vision. Don't leave this book on the shelf. Refer to it often. Read, review, highlight, and underscore key points. Place these powerful strategies and practical lessons into your life arsenal.

Throughout the remaining chapters, you will begin to rediscover your true potential to become more successful in your personal and professional endeavors. It's time to transform your thinking and maximize your efforts to reach your goals and dreams. Are you ready? No more time to waste—turn the page and let's get started!

CHAPTER 1

YOU HAVE THE KEYS...DRIVE!

*If you're still racing after your dreams, perhaps
you should pick up the pace.*

Big success! We all desire it, and we all seem to chase it. Success is something we want to consistently achieve in life, but it is more often dreamed about than experienced. At times we feel it is within our reach, but somehow it manages to escape our grasp, despite how passionate we are in our pursuits. Have you ever wondered why this happens? Achieving success requires much more than having great passion. It involves learning how to think, plan, and develop God-inspired strategies that evolve into faith-filled actions. One of the most valuable lessons I've learned is that my greatest successes did not happen by chance, but rather occurred when I intentionally involved God in my endeavors. Each venture also required an unyielding focus and a relentless work ethic to produce a successful outcome. All too often, people want to solely rely on faith as opposed to putting in a lot of sweat equity. Preparation, faith, and hard work go hand-in-hand, they all work together in complementary dimensions (James 2:14–18).[1] You should trust God, prepare yourself, and honor him by working hard. Whether it's running your own business, leading your family, advancing your career, or creating financial security, you should work hard to develop a strategy that puts you on a path that leads to the best possible results.

Life is a time-sensitive journey, and every path we choose is important. Every day is a race against the clock that requires us to drive toward our goals. We must be aware that there are no time-outs in life and sometimes you may not get second chances to make things happen. Life can change in an instant. The darkest moments in my life occurred through a series of unexpected events where I desperately wished I could have called a timeout.

I could not take a timeout when my wife agonized horribly in a fetal position in the hospital for weeks, desperately gasping for air, as she suffered from a grave lung disease that the doctors could not diagnose, even after biopsies, fluid drains, and surgery. It did not look good and we expected the worst. I stayed by her bedside, on my knees, in prayer for weeks. Out of nowhere I learned that my young, healthy, vibrant sister had suffered a stroke from an unknown heart abnormality that left her in a catatonic state…she passed. I also received news that a close relative had been charged, convicted, and sentenced to prison. My father was diagnosed with cancer and undergoing aggressive treatment while Parkinson's continued to eat away at my mother's neurological system, permanently taking away her control.

Life was stressful and complicated, and I needed a timeout, but there weren't any. I was tasked to deploy for my second combat tour in the Persian Gulf. This time I was assigned to the heart of Baghdad as one of the few remaining ground advisors before President Obama withdrew us from the country. My assignment was tough. Every day, in both my public and private life, I had to navigate through the fog and friction of war. I knew I had to remain strong because my family, those serving alongside me, and our nation was depending on me to think and lead with a clear head, especially during harassing small arms fire and improvised explosive device attacks. During this time in my life I was stressed out and fatigued and felt as if I was losing the race—I needed to catch my breath, but there were no timeouts. But, through the grace of God, I found my second wind, regained my focus, and kept charging uphill. That stretch of road in my life was bumpy and full of twists and turns, but I knew better and brighter days were ahead. I had the keys and it was up to me to continue driving forward. Those dreadful moments drew out the best in me. I grew and learned a lot about willpower and winning. No matter how bad things were, I stayed the course and kept driving forward. God helped me through it all, and I know He can help you through the rough patches of your journey.

I know life hasn't been easy for you either, but that's why you're stronger today. No matter what you face in life, you must keep driving forward toward your goals. Despite obstacles, disappointments, delays, and detours it is important to know the general course you'd like to travel and begin to drive your efforts in that direction. Every pathway presents new possibilities for you to explore and experience life beyond what you've imagined. I've come to understand that only those who are resilient and willing to pay the price will ever get the chance to experience uncommon successes in their lives. At some point, we all must decide whether we're going to step onto the fast track and race toward the lives we were destined to live, or opt to sit in the stadium stands and wonder about what could have been. The latter does not have to be your plight. Anthony Robbins once said, "The force of life is the drive for fulfillment; we all have a need to experience a life of meaning. Fulfillment can only be achieved through a pattern of living in which we focus on two spiritual needs: 1) the need to continuously grow; and 2) the need to contribute beyond ourselves in a meaningful way."[2]

Every day people fuel their competitive drive to grow and contribute in a more meaningful way. They compete with themselves to become better versions of themselves. This mentality tends to boost their performance to new levels in every area of their lives. In our society, there are no rewards for poor or average performers. In the business world, there are no hiding places. Corporations are downsizing and sculpting their workforces down to ensure only the top performers remain. For many, this has sparked a relentless drive to improve personal performance and effectiveness. It has created workplace cultures that demand bold and creative thinking for solving problems. Companies are looking for better educated, better informed, and more versatile employees. Corporations are no longer tolerating mediocrity, and because of globalization, excellence is in high demand. Globalization has literally given everyone access to the world market. So despite the size of one's company, big or small, everyone is now competing in a global marketplace, and it is a fierce battleground. Despite the volatility of world markets, many people have decided to take their destiny into their own hands and create successful small businesses that are growing daily. They haven't left things to chance. They've built solid strategies that have put them on the fast track toward living out their dreams. Why should globalization matter to you? It matters because your ideas, gifts, talents, and abilities are commodities that should be exchanged on the global market to help you prosper alongside everyone who is connected to you. So get your passport ready, pack your bags, and allow your gifts and talents to take you on an exciting journey around the world. I did it—so can you.

Today, the keys are in your hands, and it is up to you to decide where you want to go. Before you start the ignition, though, you must take the time to chart out a strategic roadmap otherwise you will wander aimlessly through the upcoming years and never reach your destination. Don't allow another day to pass without taking action toward your dreams. You must set your eyes on the checkered flags and envision yourself winning in life. It's time to innovate and push to the edge of your capabilities in the best way imaginable. This is your year to cultivate the right behaviors, habits, thoughts, and actions to begin living a wildly successful life. So, take your foot off the brake pedal, step on the accelerator, and let's pick up the pace toward your dreams!

SMALL STEPS TOWARD BIG SUCCESS

Use your competitive edge: Competition can be a great thing if it's framed from the proper perspective. You should always set goals and be willing to compete with yourself to complete them. Use every God-given talent, gift, and tool to your advantage. Employ disciplines such as prayer, fasting, and study to help you grow and overcome anything that would hinder your progress.

CHAPTER 2

KNOW YOURSELF

If you know the enemy and know yourself,
you need not fear the result of a hundred battles.
Sun Tzu, *The Art of War*

The journey of a successful life begins with knowing yourself. When you know yourself, it empowers you to slay the giants in your path and victoriously move forward toward greater things—big things you've never imagined. It has been said that we live in a world of infinite possibilities. For us to take full advantage of our true potential and all that life has to offer, we must trust ourselves, step out on the wings of probability, and take some chances. There's no exact formula for ensuring success in our endeavors, but with careful preparation and a good strategy you can decrease your margin of failure and increase the odds that you'll succeed.

Being successful is not necessarily about glory or the gold, private jets or Bugatti Veyrons; it's about the meaning and value derived from intentionality, from being in control of your life's course. It's about building strategies and leaning into opportunities in such a way that you completely change the way a situation develops. There are times when we sense that something great is pulsating deep down inside us, and that our lives will not feel accomplished until we get on the path to pursuing our true passions. Many of us believe that life has much more to offer, but our internal compass doesn't always point toward True North when we stand at the intersection of making major life decisions. When we look at our lives and the many paths it can take, it can be a nerve-racking ordeal trying to figure out what we should do next and the best way to get there. The state of not knowing what to do applies to all of us as we progress through different phases of our lives. Whether it's graduating from high school or entering into retirement, life doesn't provide a step-by-step instruction manual that tells us what our next move should be.

Maybe you've chased your dreams before, lost your footing, and *failed*, and now you don't think that you have what it takes to get back up again and make them materialize. Perhaps you've lived through much trouble and endured a long series of disappointments that have extinguished the fire in your belly for taking risks, making things happen, and solving problems. This is not uncommon and you are not alone. Life is extremely unpredictable and the solutions to our problems are not always straightforward and neatly packaged. As we grow older, we become risk averse and it becomes much easier to stay within the boundaries that we've set for ourselves. As each year passes, it becomes more frightening to leave our comfort zones and step into territory that is completely different or unknown. However, anyone who wants to be successful will keep testing their limits and break out of the cage that confines them to a life of mediocrity. If we never stretch ourselves to try new things, we'll always fall short of maximizing our true potential, and be forced to live behind the bars of regret for not making the most of our lives.

Like many, you desire to get the most out of life, but your day-to-day routine feels like nothing more than a combat survival drill. Whether it's getting through your morning exercise session, business meetings, juggling your family's schedule, or just trying to figure out what's for dinner, every day feels the same. You're constantly in a hurry, running from one thing to the next, but you're not covering much ground or getting much done. Fatigue is setting in and your body does not look or feel the same as it did a few years ago. Life is beginning to take its toll on you. Does this sound a little like your situation?

Every coin has two sides and perhaps you're on the opposite side of this coin and you have it all together. Let me be the first to congratulate you on your success! You may have a college education, a great family, a promising career, financial independence, and you're running with perfect form at marathon pace. Things are working out well, but lingering deep down in your core, in the private recesses of your soul, you still feel a little empty and discontent. You like the results of what you've been able to achieve in your lifetime, but you don't necessarily envision yourself doing those things for the rest of your life. You feel that you have more to do, more to contribute to the world. Does any of this describe your current reality? If so, it's time to take an honest approach and look more closely at your life and what you would really like to do with it to thrive and feel more alive.

While our experiences have helped shape us into who we are today, that does not necessarily mean that we know who we are, what we're passionate about, or what we desire out of life. Knowing yourself is the process of understanding who you are beneath the surface. It goes beyond knowing your favorite color or favorite song. With the deepest sense of humility, when you know yourself, you are brought face-to-face with your public strengths and private insecurities. Knowing yourself helps you to be confident and comfortable with who you are and what you can bring to the table. Once you tap into the confidence that flows within you, you'll be able to stay calm, cool, and collected even in the worst situations.

Knowing yourself also cues you in to your limitations and to when you should ask God and others for help. The scriptures assure us that God is our refuge and strength, an ever-present help in trouble.[3] You can't do everything on your own. This is why we must invite God into our affairs. Sometimes you'll need to recruit a team to help you with some of the heavy lifting. Just look at Jesus's example, he recruited twelve men to help him carry his message of redemption to the world. He said to them, "Follow me, and I will make you fishers of men." (Matthew 4:19) (NKJV). He displayed no hubris in asking people to follow and assist him in his efforts. If Jesus needed assistance in achieving his goals, surely we might need assistance in our endeavors as well. When you possess this level of self-knowledge, it can be used as a powerful tool to kick- start making positive changes that will consistently lead to big success in life. Furthermore, it helps you improve your plans for the future because you become more in tune with your core strengths and weaknesses. Let's take a look at a few actions that you can take to help you get to know yourself better.

EVALUATE YOUR REACTIONS

No one knows you better than you. Let's be honest. You and I both know that there are times when we let our emotions get the best of us. You may be a person who shuts down when criticized, or you may be a person who rises to the challenge when you're told that you can't do certain things. As an adult, you may still find yourself reacting to the past. Maybe you react from guilt about past mistakes, or still feel bothered by things that occurred during your childhood or in previous relationships. Sometimes you're able to maintain your poise, but other days you might just flip out! In most cases our emotional reactions stem from our own needs, fears, and unresolved issues.

When we evaluate our reactions it helps us see ourselves as the outside world sees us and helps us move forward with success. It's one thing to know how you've reacted, but it's altogether different when you know the reasons why you've reacted that way. We all encounter heartaches, hurt feelings, frustration, and pain. The key is to realize that it's not about what happens, but rather how you respond to things. The intensity of our emotional reactions varies from person to person and often influence the way others view our character. The way we react can stem from our personality traits and the environment we grew up in, but it doesn't excuse our behavior when we react in the wrong manner. From an introspective point, our reactions can clue us in to our own level of discipline and self-control when we're under stress. They can also determine how successful we can be when we're working under pressure or with other people.

As a military leader, I had to learn that we are frequently thermostats—not thermometers. Leaders often operate under constant pressure and scrutiny. They are expected not to have bad days. In my professional life, I didn't realize how my reactions and mood set the atmosphere for my front office staff. Let's face it, whenever the boss walks into the office and slams the door behind himself, it can cause ripple effects throughout the organization. Emotions are contagious. Many of your subordinates will spend unnecessary time trying to figure out what or who upset you, and the best way to respond to it. This is counterproductive because we need our staff to feel comfortable in their working environment by not having to tiptoe around on eggshells because of our mood. The same principles apply for leaders in the home; when mom or dad is upset, it sets the mood and temperature for the entire house. As I digress, let me offer a little bit of advice for men in relationships: if momma is happy, your house will be happy. Take the time to make momma smile—trust me, it will pay off! Your home should always be a fun and peaceful sanctuary.

Of course there will be moments when tempers flare and emotions run high, but you should always strive to never let people see you react in an out-of-control manner. There will be other instances where you'll need to show carefully controlled anger to place the proper emphasis on a problem area, but it should always conclude on a positive note. With this in mind, how will you react in your business and home environment to help you achieve your vision of success? How will you contribute toward creating healthy and peaceful atmospheres to work and live in?

We should frequently engage in a bit of soul-searching to figure out our trigger points, hot buttons, and fears and develop ways to counteract them. One of my bosses once told me that when he had heated reactions during arguments with others, he would calm himself by repeating in his head over and over again, "It doesn't matter, it doesn't matter, it doesn't matter." And soon he would calm down, reset his attitude, and be able to finish his conversations with balanced restraint. When you know your reactions, you can positively use your emotions to negotiate any situation with dignity and class.

KNOW YOUR DESIRES

Many people determine their desires based on the cookie-cutter notion of the American Dream or what their parents or others have desired for them. Some may resort to a list of things that fall into the categories of power, money, and fame. The more they have, the more they want, the better they feel. Others may strive to attain good health, happiness, fulfillment, or some other gratifying emotional reward, and for them, that is enough. And yet, others may decide to commit themselves to a lifetime of public service to benefit humanity in general. We all desire different things in life and nothing is wrong with that. We are entitled to our personal preferences, opinions, and desires. With that being said, "What do you really desire in life?"

Some people can concisely and clearly articulate what they want in life, but for others it takes some time to figure out. It's similar to having a craving for something to eat, but not knowing exactly what you want until all the choices are laid out before you. At a restaurant you might study the menu; at home you might dive deeply into the refrigerator or pantry. You search and search and the entire time you're subconsciously checking off all the things that you do not want. After a while, you might begin to narrow your focus down to what you really desire. Once you've found something that will satisfy your craving, factors such as cost, preparation time, or potential consequences to your health may affect your final decision—but it still does not change your initial desire.

The same is true with life. Sometimes we don't exactly know what we desire from life's menu, but we do know that we're hungry for something greater. Many of us spend our lives checking off all the things we do not want, finding all the reasons we can't have what we truly desire. When we consider the cost of making things happen, the time it will take, and the possible consequences, we often remove valid desires from our list and settle for less satisfying alternatives. As our search continues, we end up doing things that are not fulfilling, and we never truly satisfy our life-long cravings. However, successful people know what they want and they stay hungry for it! They want things that add value and strength to their lives. They don't allow cost, time, preparation, or potential consequences to spoil their appetites. They use their hunger to develop moral strategies to go after the good and righteous things that they crave. Over the years, I've learned that God will feed your hunger for success only to the capacity that you have to receive it. He is a God of provision and will feed and fill our spirits as well as our natural bodies. He provides us with assurance in the scriptures that, "blessed are they which do hunger and thirst after righteousness for they shall be filled." (Matthew 5:6). With that being said, we should desire our lives to be filled with complete joy and satisfaction.

Now, I would be irresponsible if I didn't mention how we can develop a desire for good things, and if we're not careful, it can lead to overindulgence. Like any good diet, your desires should be balanced.

There are times when we allow our desires to override good decision making. For example, sometimes we'll rationalize with ourselves as to why we really need that thick slice of strawberry cheesecake after each meal. We'll say, "I'll just run a few extra minutes on the treadmill or do a few more crunches to burn it off." Or, during shopping trips, we'll make statements like, "I really need those Jimmy Choo pumps and the Michael Kors purse", even though you know they're outside of your budget and you have hundreds of shoes and purses already in your closet with price tags on them. We rationalize our decisions by saying, "I'll only live once, so I'm going to enjoy it!" Then later, when you step on the scale or go to the ATM, you become an emotional wreck because you've gained a few extra pounds and your funds are insufficient. I'm not suggesting that you shouldn't enjoy certain creature comforts in life; I *am* saying that you should control your desires in a healthy and responsible way...maybe eat one thin slice of pie and then save up for the pumps and handbag. That way you do not have to live with the regrets linked to compulsive behavior or overindulgence.

KNOW YOUR SELF-WORTH

We were all born with a distinct sense of self-awareness. Self-awareness helps us understand our own uniqueness, strengths, weaknesses, and potentials. It also gives us insight into knowing when things are not working for us, even if they've worked for us in the past. Research has shown that self-awareness starts to emerge around our first year of life and becomes much more developed around eighteen months. It can be influenced by our environments, cultures, upbringings, or personalities. As we grow older, we can begin to develop a hyper or heightened sense of self-awareness and begin to veer into self-consciousness. While self-awareness and self-consciousness are closely related, be careful not to confuse the two. Self-consciousness usually springs forth from worries about certain physical features, inadequacies, limitations, shortcomings, etc. It can be fueled by what we believe about ourselves and by what we believe others think of us. We are all a little self-conscious about certain things. For instance, if you're standing in a group and someone wipes their nose or checks their face, you automatically begin to check your own nose and face. We pick up their cues and take action subconsciously to protect ourselves from potential embarrassment, even when our nose and face are perfectly fine. We do this because at one point we might have walked around with something in our nose or on our face and wondered why no one told us about it. You felt embarrassed. So now you become self-conscious about these things when you're in public settings. Am I right? This is normal, but we must not become so self-conscious about our shortcomings that it prevents us from moving forward in life.

Self-worth is defined as a sense of one's own value or worth as a person. It often indicates a person's level of self-esteem and self-respect. These attitudes are intrinsic components that we must wholly understand in order to come to terms with who we really are. When we know who we are it boosts our self-esteem and gives us confidence to overcome our limitations and succeed. Sometimes we can be our worst critics, but we must learn to appreciate ourselves and value our capabilities. We should be cognizant that the way we view and respect ourselves often affects how other people view and respect us. We shouldn't expect people to love or respect us when we do not love or respect ourselves. We teach people how to treat us by what we tolerate. Many people find themselves in toxic relationships because they did not respect themselves enough to realize that they deserved better. We must set boundaries for our lives and our relationships by setting a righteous standard of dignity and respect.

When we determine our self-worth it enables us to believe that we are capable of producing the best outcome possible with our innate gifts and talents. In order to succeed and stand out among our peers, we must know where our most valuable gifts and strengths lie. With humility, it gives us the satisfaction of knowing that we are treasured and respected as decent individuals. Every few years I take personality tests comprised of multiple choice questions that help me to learn about how I view my own self-worth, personality, and how I come across to others. These tests help me to understand more about my levels of pessimism, optimism, preferences, and inclinations. There are many different types of personality tests online such as the Myers-Briggs Type Indicator that will help aid you in your journey of self-discovery. Perhaps you should try one for yourself.

Persist Until Success Happens
Life Application Exercise

1. Using my previous food selection example in the last chapter, let's do a drill. First, ask yourself the question, "What do I want in life?" Take a moment to jot down all the things you want, regardless of how trivial or superficial they seem. Next, ask yourself, "Why do I want these things?" If you discover that they do not add value to your life, or will not bring you sustained happiness—remove them from your list. With the remaining list that you have, begin ranking your desires according to those that matter most. Now consider the cost, time, and sacrifices you'll need to make in order to get them. Do any of these factors change your decision or desires? If they do, remove them from your list. If they do not, start building consistent strategies to move toward getting what you want in life.

2. Take a moment to help discover who you really are by taking an assessment. Here are a few online Web site links:
   - http://www.my-personality-test.com/personality-type/
   - http://www.mbtionline.com/

3. Here are a few more thoughtful questions that you might ask yourself in order to find out what you would like to do in life: What sacrifices am I willing to make to get what I desire? What are my greatest achievements so far? Who do I admire most and why do I admire them? What am I passionate about? If I had unlimited resources what would I do and where would I go?

SMALL STEPS TOWARD BIG SUCCESS

Be honest with yourself: Self-awareness involves knowing your strengths and weaknesses. When you are realistic and honest about yourself and the goals you have set, it indicates you are growing as an individual. Don't spend time hiding behind masks to cover your weaknesses, but search for ways to improve on them little by little.

CHAPTER 3

TRANSFORM YOUR THINKING

Master your thoughts…master your life.

Our lives can be so demanding and stressful that maintaining our sanity can become an overwhelming challenge. Throughout our day we allow so many things to occupy our headspace that we do not have much room left to think clearly. Sometimes we begin to zone out during the day and have trouble sleeping at night because our mind is stampeding with ideas, thoughts, issues, worries, and questions…at the wrong time. This can be exhausting, especially when thoughts tend to pass through our minds without much order or purpose. On the flip side it can be a good thing when we're allowing our creative juices to flow, but it can also be quite distracting and nerve-racking when we can't concentrate.

As long as humans exist, there will be a market for repairing and renewing the mind. Depression is on the rise, therapists' appointment calendars are full, and more people are on mental health medications than ever before. Some have veered away from traditional approaches to getting mental help and have plunged head first (pun intended) into less-invasive options. Life coaching is the latest rave; coaches assist their clients in creative ways to help them gain clarity, maximize their potential, and build better lives. The difference between therapists and coaches is that therapists are often doctors whereas life coaches are like personal trainers. While I can see legitimate value in both, I recommend that you do research about each and take the approach that best suits your needs. They can both put you on a path toward discovering your purpose and help engineer a better way to live.

The United Negro College Fund's motto rings so true when it exclaims that "a mind is a terrible thing to waste." In our current age, there is much talk about how to detox our bodies to live healthier and longer, but there is little talk about how to detox our minds. We often worry about things we cannot control. We fret about our jobs, finances, health, relationships, and so on. We have a tendency to major on minor things, adding more stress and anxiety to our hectic lives. I've heard the saying that, "worry is like a rocking chair, it keeps you busy but never gets you anywhere." Many people spend countless hours contemplating worst-case scenarios over and over in their heads, each time building up anxiety (and stomach acid) over what they think an outcome will be. As things grow worse, they begin to nourish negative thoughts while drawing catastrophic conclusions to questions, such as "Why do things around me keep falling apart? Why do terrible things keep happening to me and the people I love? Why do all of my relationships end in ruin?" Does any of this sound familiar to you?

Throughout history, statesmen, poets, and philosophers have disagreed on many things, but many are in unanimous agreement on one point: "We become what we think about." Proverbs 23:7 states, "For as he thinketh in his heart, so is he." In essence, the way you think reveals who you are now, and determines who you will become.

The Roman emperor Marcus Aurelius put it this way: "Our life is what our thoughts make of it."

One Saturday afternoon, a cranky old business owner was visiting his family. As he lay down to take a nap, his great nephew decided to have a little fun by putting Limburger cheese on his uncle's mustache. Soon the old man awoke with a snort and charged out of the bedroom, saying, "This room stinks." Through the house he went, finding that every room smelled the same. Desperately he made his way outside only to find that "the whole world stinks!" The same is true when we fill our minds with negativity that we are not willing to release. If we do not release negative thoughts, everything we experience and everybody we encounter will smell like the scent that we hold in our mind. This occurs most often when someone has gone through a traumatic experience or bad relationship.

In most cases, the questions we ask and the things we hold in our minds stem from overactive imaginations, our attitudes, or latent fears we have about situations we assume are inescapable. It can cause us to wake up drenched in cold sweat from nightmares that torment our minds as we sleep. If we do not find a way to flush out these thoughts and continue to allow them to attach to a crisis we are going through, we are more likely to pick up even more toxic thoughts and behavior. Typically the things we fear most are imagined, but they still have a real effect on us. In other instances, our fears may actually be legitimate, but we haven't figured out a way to cope with them. Ralph Waldo Emerson once said, "A man is what he thinks about all day long." The powerful truth is, what we think "influences our own reality." Any thought that is left unchecked is established as truth inside of us. This can be good or bad depending on how you've channeled your thoughts.

A negative mind will never give you a positive life. All thoughts are birthed from our creative impulses which involve various areas of the brain. In order to think with more clarity, we must strive to be more positive than negative. One problem with negative thoughts is that they often form below your conscious level of awareness. They run like scripts in the background, similar to how many computer programs operate. Sometimes we attempt to suppress them or find other outlets to take our minds off of them. If we don't correctly process them, sooner or later tension begins to mount and we emotionally short circuit. If we're not careful, we can surrender to our thoughts and begin to permanently harbor negative ideas in our minds that are psychologically damaging. We must learn to disagree with negative thoughts that form during the conversations we have in our heads.

GETTING PAROLED FROM A LIFE SENTENCE

Countless men and women suffer from what I refer to as "mental bondage." This occurs when your mind is imprisoned by negative thoughts that confine you to a life of isolation, discouragement, and pain. When your thoughts embrace negativity and emotional pain, it indicates that your mind is refusing to be healthy. When the mind refuses to be healthy, it becomes dis-eased, and the body soon follows.

Mental bondage can become a lifelong warden, preventing a person from ever experiencing freedom in life. Simply put, it can cause people to become enslaved to seeking the approval of others. It can cause one to spend the majority of their life thinking that they'll never measure up. They become unsure about their place in the world and devote much of their time and energy searching for new ways to validate and prove their value. Some chase after artificial acceptance and become miserable and lost in the pursuit. Many tend to live under the illusion of "If only I did this or had this, made the right connection, became like so-and-so, then I would be happy." At some point in our lives, we have all have suffered hurt or rejection.

For some, our deepest and most painful hurt has come from those who should have encouraged and loved us the most. If you are battling with insecurity and rejection, you must choose by faith to break the chains of seeking man's approval. This will put you on the path to experiencing true happiness and joy.

True happiness emerges at the moment we discover our value. It germinates from the way we think of ourselves. When we are happy it releases endorphins, it liberates our minds and gives us the freedom to think more positively and productively. Happiness occurs when you learn to conduct your *own* appraisal of life and get excited about the great things you can do and achieve. We all have the God-given right to be happy, so why do we continue to shackle this privilege? Sometimes we shackle our happiness by making unhealthy comparisons of ourselves with others. This is unwise. You should always measure your progress by how far you've come, rather than how far along others think you should be. You must strip yourself of old ideas and opinions that others have concerning your life and your future. If this sounds a little like your situation, it's time for you to get paroled and experience real happiness and freedom in life.

There are a few ways to do this. First, you must heighten your situational awareness to recognize when you're slipping into a subconscious state of worry and negativity. Pay attention to your emotions. If you notice that you're feeling a little irritable, cynical, or stressed you may be subconsciously harboring negative thoughts. Challenge and check those thoughts that keep you stuck in a miserable shame spiral. Conducting attitude checks throughout the day can help alleviate these sudden shifts in your mood and help guard your thinking. You're most vulnerable when you are tired, busy, and haven't been able to read the Bible.

Another way to guard your thinking is by replacing negative thoughts with prayer, devotion, singing hymns and songs of worship, and meditation on the word of God. This keeps your mind stable and free from toxic ideas, thoughts, and images. The more you spend time practicing these biblical disciplines, the more God begins to renew your mind. Slowly but surely, the mental images that are stored in your mind will transform into the positive portrait that God is painting for your future.

You should frequently monitor your pattern of thinking and refresh your thoughts by quoting passages of scripture. The apostle Paul tells us to "fix your thoughts on what is true, and honorable, and right, and pure, and lovely, and admirable. Think about things that are excellent and worthy of praise."[4] Quoting scripture helps keep your thoughts pure and under control.

Controlling how you think, and what you think, gives you the winning edge throughout life. Your thoughts fuel your actions and expose the depth of your character when you are faced with challenges. Generally speaking, your thoughts are the final frontier of your privacy and the birthplace of your creativity. They should be channeled toward creating good strategies to beat the odds and reach goals in life. Your thoughts should be positive, vibrant, and filled with healthy expectations. Most important, they should be filtered with truth, honesty, justice, purity, loveliness, and goodness.

Let me reiterate, true transformation begins with the mind. The apostle Paul tells us in Romans 12:2, "Do not conform to the pattern of this world, but be transformed by the renewing of your mind. Then you will be able to test and approve what God's will is—his good, pleasing and perfect will." The Message Bible states it this way, "Don't become so well-adjusted to your culture that you fit into it without even thinking. Instead, fix your attention on God. You'll be changed from the inside out." Ephesians 4:22—24 says we should "throw off our old sinful nature and our former way of life, which is corrupted by lust and deception. Instead, let the Spirit renew your thoughts and attitudes. Put on your new nature, created to be like God—truly righteous and holy."[5] The thread of continuity that exists between these scriptures is that we must invite God into our minds in order to change our way of reasoning and consequently our behavior. By doing so we can help change our lives as well as the lives of others. We find the apostle Paul again in 2 Corinthians 10:4, declaring that "we use God's mighty weapons, not worldly weapons, to knock down the strongholds of human reasoning and to destroy false arguments." We destroy every proud obstacle that keeps people from knowing God. We capture their rebellious thoughts and teach them to obey Christ." Hal Lindsey points out that "to renew" means to exchange one thing for another. In other words, when we put off and put on, we're exchanging our thinking for God's. If we're not willing to yield, set aside and relinquish our own thoughts, our thinking process will never be renewed and our lives will never be transformed.[6]

My beloved, God has a plan for you and things will come together sooner than you think. The gospel according to Matthew records the words of Jesus this way: "Therefore do not worry, saying, 'What shall we eat?' or 'What shall we drink?' or 'What shall we wear?' For after all these things the Gentiles seek. For your heavenly Father knows that you need all these things. But seek first the kingdom of God and His righteousness, and all these things shall be added to you. Therefore do not worry about tomorrow..."[7]

Persist Until Success Happens
Life Application Exercise

1. Practice mindfulness and stop saying negative things about yourself out loud.

2. Start saying positive things and repeat them to yourself out loud. *Do this all day about everything.*

3. Start replacing negative thoughts with prayer, devotion, singing hymns and songs of worship, and meditation on the word of God.

SMALL STEPS TOWARD BIG SUCCESS

Shift your thinking: If you find yourself feeling doubtful about your abilities, try engaging in a little bit of encouraging self-talk. For example, you might say, "I am smart, innovative, and fully gifted! I can do all things through Christ who gives me strength!" This helps cleanse the mind, keeping it in a positive and healthy state. With that said, will you change "stinking" thinking and start using your mind to produce creativity instead of negativity? I believe you can, and I believe that with God you will!

CHAPTER 4

GOALED MIND OF FAILURE

*It is difficult to climb the ladder of success
when you're afraid of heights!*

Failure is an often misunderstood ingredient to character development and success. Many people are terrified to step out into the unknown because they fear failure. The problem is that most people view failure as an ending point rather than a stepping stone on the path to success. This may sound strange, but in some cases, the thought of achieving success and performing at higher levels literally frightens people. They become consumed by the consequence of doing poorly. This fear causes them to subconsciously sabotage their chances of future success.

Experiencing failure can induce doubt or cause you to question your self-worth, goals, and ambitions. I've had subordinates who refused to do what it took to be promoted because they feared assuming the responsibilities of a higher rank. Their fear of failing stifled their potential, leaving them void of the courage to rise to the occasion on behalf of the people who counted on them most.

It is difficult to climb the ladder of success when you're afraid of heights! The overwhelming pressure to succeed can cause even the greatest competitor to choke and never rise to their true potential. Thoughts such as, "What happens if I fail?" or "What if this doesn't work?" tend to stall their minds and keep them from stepping up their performance to the next level. This kind of thinking can cause us to abort our takeoff and never leave the runway as we sit and watch others soar above us. You should never give up or abort your dreams, especially when you know that you have more effort to give.

Once there was a frog hopping around a farmyard, when it decided to investigate the barn. Being somewhat careless, and maybe a little too curious, he ended up falling into a pail half-filled with fresh milk. As he clambered about attempting to get out, he found that the sides of the pail were too high and steep to reach the top. He tried to stretch his back legs to push off the bottom of the pail but it was too deep. But this frog was determined not to give up, and he continued to struggle. He kicked and squirmed and kicked and squirmed, until at last, all his churning about in the milk had turned the milk into a big hunk of butter. The butter was now solid enough for him to climb onto and get out of the pail! The moral of the story is to never give up no matter what your situation.

To fly high in life we must unstick our minds, overcome the stage fright that precedes possible failure—and never give up. When we fall into various situations our fear can induce what some refer to as "situational paralysis." Situational paralysis is when we become so frightened by a challenging situation that we do not respond at all, almost like a deer in headlights. It is a crippling moment of indecision—a moment when we become stuck rather than liberated through our power to act. It is when a person waits for something or someone else to change their situation before deciding to take action to produce the change that is needed. It's the result of thinking of the situation as a threat, rather than seeing a new opportunity emerge.

At some point we must face our fears, learn to anticipate what will happen next and adapt to changing situations. This will provide us with the boost that we need in order to get unstuck.

DEVELOP FROM THE NEGATIVES

Back in the mid-1970s, my father would set up family photo shoots during special occasions. He had an old Polaroid instant camera stored in the top of his closet that he would occasionally dust off to capture magical family moments. There were no such things as front facing cell phone cameras and selfies back then.

It was during these times that my four siblings and I would get dressed up in our good Sunday outfits (starched and pressed of course) to take family photos. My older brother and I were as sharp as thumb tacks as we sported elephant ear-sized bowties and had natural parts in our hair that were wider than a four-lane highway. Our afros would glisten from thick Royal Crown pomade as we waited at high noon for the photo shoot to begin. Like clockwork, and in drill sergeant manner, our father would align us against the picturesque backdrop of our rickety chain link fence then tell us to say, "CHEESE." He'd snap the picture and the camera would spit out a square piece of paper with a faintly colored image on it. Years ago, Polaroid camera film used a special type of developing sheet that produced the negative first, and after about a minute, the positive or finished photo image would develop.

As little kids, we weren't too thrilled about taking pictures outside in the scorching Georgia sun, but we were excited about who was going to shake the photo once the camera ejected the print. We were under the impression that by taking the photo into a dark shaded area and waving it back and forth in a fanning motion we would speed up the development of the negative. We would grab the print from our dad and shake the negative until the obscure image became clearer and clearer. After a minute or so of fanning and shaking, bright colors would burst through, and the images would gradually gain definition. At last, the complete picture would suddenly appear—clear and in full detail!

There is a lot to be learned about the nature of God in my example. God often uses "negative" moments, "dark places," and "shaking" to develop the portrait of our lives. There are times when he hides us inside trouble—he takes us into the dark room of life. He puts us in a place of isolation where we must depend on him to bring us through. You may even ask yourself, "Why has God quarantined me? What has He done by casting me in this dark place?" What you must understand is, there is a higher truth that God reveals out of our situations. The truth is that he is helping us to grow in faith.

I once read a billboard sign that beautifully captured the essence of how we should develop the negatives in our life. It read:

"Life is like a camera. Focus on what is important.
Capture the good times. Develop from the negatives.
And if things don't work out, take another shot."

Impossible dreams are being realized by ordinary people who have remained disciplined enough to surf the waves of setback and find value in their failures. The truth is that anyone who has experienced major success has also had to recover from their fair share of negative moments. It is said that after being cut from his high school basketball team, Michael Jordan went home, locked himself in his room and cried his eyeballs out. Shortly after, he harnessed his emotions and allowed his tears to become the liquid catalyst for his competitive fire as he went on to become a six-time NBA Champion, five-time MVP and four-time All-star and Hall of Fame inductee. Jordan said, "I've missed more than 9,000 shots in my career. I've lost almost 300 games. Twenty-six times, I've been trusted to take the game winning shot and missed. I've failed over and over and over again in my life. And that is why I succeed."[8]

In another example, it has been said that Albert Einstein was not able to speak until he was almost four years old and that his teachers said he would never amount to much. Apparently Einstein had a hearing problem as well because he failed to listen to the cynical comments of his teachers and went on to become an iconic theoretical physicist and Nobel Prize winner.[9]

And at thirty years old, Steve Jobs was left devastated and depressed after being brusquely removed from the company he started. He bounced back, however, and became the cofounder of both Apple Inc. and Pixar Animation Studios.[10] The world as we know it has reaped historical benefits from the tenacity and instinctive will to succeed that these individuals demonstrated. To increase our own chances of overcoming our failures, we must be willing to be a little uncomfortable and develop the right habits so we can live without the regrets that come from not trying. I'm sure you've heard it before: "If at first you don't succeed, try, try again." This may sound like juvenile advice, but it is extremely practical when you're experiencing frustration from disappointments.

Life's greatest challenges produce opportunities for tremendous growth and development. It is from the wellspring of negative experiences that we're able to draw wisdom and insight about how to live better. Without the negatives in our lives, our progression stagnates. When negatives are absent, we tend to hibernate in a cave of complacency allowing our true potential to lie dormant and unchallenged. If we view negative experiences as our personal life coach guiding us toward happiness and hope, we will soon experience valuable transformation in our lives.

Your negative experiences can be used as value based life-learning experiences that let you know what you need to do to change direction. If you allow God to transform your mind during the process, the negative snapshots will eventually become clear and you'll begin to see the complete imagery of your destiny—bold, beautiful, and in living color.

TAKE THE LIMITS OFF

For months my youngest daughter tried to overcome her grave fear of performing an unassisted back handspring. For weeks on end at the gym she tried to do a back handspring but wasn't able to land it unassisted. She had been taught the proper technique, but was afraid of jumping backward while having to support her own weight. After watching multiple YouTube videos and seeing her friends "bust it," she still could not build up the confidence to do the movement on her own.

Every Wednesday at tumbling practice she used the tumbling wedges and did back walkovers on the trampoline. She also tried to bribe me into buying a trampoline. Needless to say, she soon fell behind her peers as they moved on to more advanced techniques. I could not understand why she was having such a hard time with this movement.

After all, when I was her age I learned to do multiple back handsprings without taking a single lesson. Creatively inspired by Kung Fu movies, my friends and I learned gymnastics at our own risk in the backyard (without safety nets or tumbling mats). We would do a back tuck off the top of a car's trunk or some other raised structure and stick the landing perfectly. Surprisingly enough, no one was ever seriously injured. But no amount of encouragement or persuasion was going to sway my daughter to do an unassisted back handspring, even in a safe environment. I even went to the extreme of dusting off my talents to show her that a man of nearly forty years old still had what it took to perform this technique. I landed the back handspring with no problems in our front yard in Okinawa, Japan. I'm sure you can find a clip of it somewhere on social media.

I came to the realization that my daughter was harboring fears that she wasn't willing to release. Her fears had become deeply rooted in her subconscious mind and put a damper on her performance. She had encountered a mental block that prevented her from executing the movement. Sometimes the only limitations that exist in our minds are the ones that we placed there. Despite my demonstration and example as a parent, she would have to overcome her fears on her own and assume the risk in order to reap the reward. I could not do it for her. I learned that the only thing that was going to help her overcome her fear was trial, errors, and time.

She needed to fall a few times to overcome her fear of jumping backward. One day she finally built up the courage and asked me to spot her. I spotted her on the first few attempts and she was able to perform the movement perfectly. Once I saw that she was gaining confidence, I pretended to spot her and moved my hands away as she jumped backward and she landed on her shoulder. She immediately burst out into laughter! She realized that a botched tumble wasn't the end of the world. The same is true in life. Sometimes we'll fall and have botched tumbles, but it's up to us to decide whether to laugh, cry, or do both. Once she overcame her fear, she was able to move forward in her training by not being afraid to jump backward. She kept practicing and she finally nailed her back handspring. She finally took the limits off.

FROM FRUSTRATION TO INNOVATION

Many of the technological advancements that we enjoy today would not have come to fruition if inventors allowed their frustrations to spoil their innovation. They pressed through their setbacks and found value in their failures. After hundreds of tests and retests they discovered that a failed test led them to success.

Sometimes frustration sets in and causes us to view some problems as being unsolvable. Every problem has a solution; but the solution is often buried beneath frustration resulting from fruitless attempts to find answers. I've learned that when you're frustrated your thinking becomes foggy and hinders your ability see the problem clearly. This is when you should stop everything and carefully examine what you've done wrong so you can get on the path to doing it right. As hard as it may be to suffer a setback, recognize that you can pick up the pieces and move on! Prime Minister Winston Churchill summed it up this way, "Success is going from failure to failure without losing enthusiasm." Such was the case with Thomas Edison.

Thomas Edison failed more than one thousand times when trying to create the light bulb. This story is often told as five thousand or ten thousand times depending on the version. When asked about it, Edison allegedly said, "I have not failed one thousand times. I have successfully discovered one thousand ways to NOT make a light bulb." In other words, through failed tests he now had more knowledge about why his previous ideas did not work. After exhausting multiple options, Edison found himself closer to the solution. He changed his way of thinking about the problem and stretched his creativity to new levels to find the right answers. His setbacks proved to be invaluable opportunities to learn. This became an exciting notion for Edison and it can become an exciting notion for you as well. Think about how much you learned from your failures and how close you are to success. You're just one spark away from a bright future.

Everyone fails from time to time and, typically, emotional turmoil follows. During these seasons we must wrap ourselves in bands of resiliency and bounce back from letdowns. We must learn to correctly manage our emotions and wisely process our failures. This helps reprogram our thoughts, ideas, and actions for future success. Reversing a downward spiral takes a bit of effort and a little time, but trust me, you can do it!

It is easy to make excuses when we fail, but don't make excuses—just execute. Go into recovery mode and rise up from the ashes of failure. Allow the old cliché that "If it doesn't kill you, it makes you stronger" to resonate in your spirit. When we experience our greatest failures it produces testimonies of significant personal growth and development.

You must continue to fight through frustrating times when nothing seems to work. Remember that each round of the fight has a time that it is set to end. During your fight, don't despise being backed into a corner of failure. The corner helps you reset, and fortifies you for the next round. In the corner of failure you learn secrets for sustainment, regain stability, and develop countermeasures for the attacks. It's a place of decision-making where you may opt to surrender to the challenge or muster the courage of a true champion. Just keep calm, listen to the voice of your corner man Jesus Christ, employ his divine strategies and you will win the fight. We should use our failures to reframe, reflect on, and reset our strategies.

We can reframe the failure by getting to the root cause of our setbacks. Understanding the root cause can help us avoid making the same mistakes twice as well as identify new opportunities to improve our plans. Furthermore, failures can also push us to reflect as we determine what can be done better the next time around. Sometimes it takes failing to help us see that some of our habits and approaches are counterproductive. Finally, our failures give us time to reset. There are times when we need to step away from our failures and clear our minds. Often we are so consumed with finding an immediate fix that we don't take the time to breathe through our nose again.

Strive to find the value in your failures and see them as foundation stones that setup better options. It is time for you to reverse life's course and get back on track with believing that failure isn't final. Extract your strategies from the divine playbook (the Bible) and allow the Holy Spirit to coach you through each quarter of this season. There is no room to carry the pain of failure from your past into this new season. Keep pressing and maintain focus, because today's trials will become tomorrow's trophies! You can do all things through Christ! Live with the expectation that you will succeed and win in all areas.

Persist Until Success Happens
Life Application Exercise

1. Take a moment to write down a few things that you've learned from past failures.

2. How can you take these lessons learned and apply them to your future.

3. What was the root cause of these failures?

4. Which goals do you need to re-examine?

SMALL STEPS TOWARD BIG SUCCESS

Think outside the box: As we climb the ladder of success, the knowledge that we gain on the previous level can be applied on the next level, but it often requires expansion. As you progress up the ladder, things become more complex. This requires that you move beyond the outer parameters of thought to come up with better solutions and ideas. In other words you will have to think things through much more carefully, thoroughly, and broadly, as each decision can potentially affect your outcomes in drastic ways.

CHAPTER 5

THE POWER OF EXPECTATION

*If you do not expect anything out of life, you should
never be disappointed if nothing happens!*

E very day that you wake up presents a set of challenges that
are tailor made especially for you. There will be days that you
hit the snooze button a few times before struggling to pull
yourself out of bed and into your morning routine when you'd much
rather crawl back into the blissful comfort of your cozy bed. As you
concoct your caffeinated brew of choice to kick start your day, you
might pause to think about how you are going to deal with unresolved issues or difficult people at home or on the job. The more you
think about it, curling up in your pajamas seems like an ideal way
to handle the challenges that face you in the day ahead. You'd love
to just lounge around for the day, but the bills have to be paid and
you've got things to do!

On the other hand, if you have pleasant things to look forward
to in the upcoming day (and your Starbucks is blended correctly),
you gain a little pep in your step! You might even start humming a
little tune. Just think about how amazing you feel after waking up

to find a thoughtfully written note on your pillow from your spouse. Does it light up your morning? Your efforts to face the day become charged with new energy and excitement, despite any complex issues you may be dealing with. It is the tiny drops of happiness that create a positive ripple effect in our mood and set up our success for the day. And, when you front-load your morning with positive practices like prayer, meditation, and exercise, you set the right tone for facing the world!

All things considered, the true determining factor in how your day will unfold is enveloped within how you shape your expectations. This is also true for the sum of your life existence. Your life is shaped by what you have learned from past experiences; what you think about your present situation, and what you expect to happen in your future.

For example, during our formative years we dream up wonderful images of what we expect our lives to become as adults. For many of us, we typically envision ourselves graduating from high school or college and choosing an exciting career. For others, this comes as a package deal that includes plans to marry the perfect mate, purchase a dream home, and start a family. But life changing events such as an unplanned pregnancy (having to raise the child alone), dropping out of school with enormous debt from student loans, or going through a divorce can drastically change our plans and expectations for the future.

It can be tough to expect good things when you are currently broken and gathering the fragments of a failed relationship, project, or business venture. It can be even tougher to expect positive things tomorrow, especially when today's drama has not been resolved. The residue from past fiascos can be difficult to remove, and sometimes the consequences of a stained past can haunt us for years. They can permanently jade our perspective, making it difficult to see a bright future because of a dark reality.

Truth is, sometimes circumstances can be just right to make us to give up. When things do not happen when or how we expect them to, we might become depressed and refuse to take on the burden of trying again. As a result, our lives begin to dissolve with regret and shame. This can also cause us to compare our lives with others, which is always a losing proposition.

If you are a person that is driven by results, it can be difficult to appreciate the growth that occurs from facing challenging situations. During these moments, it's important to recognize that you frame your success by the way you respond to life. Here's a nugget of truth Viktor E. Frankl once said, "Between stimulus and response, there is a space. In that space is our power to choose our response. In our response lies our growth and our freedom."

Our minds are the processing center for decision-making. Our decisions determine our future. By and large, we tend to make decisions based on what we think or feel. In many cases, the way you think or feel about a situation foreshadows how you are going to respond. It is your response to people, to your environment and circumstances that enables you to soar above challenging situations. We often tend to react first and think later, not realizing that if we take a moment to think, we'll know how to respond to situations more appropriately. I've learned to filter my thoughts before they become words. Taking a moment to think before responding spares me from embarrassing moments, later regret, and future apologies!

EXPECT TO WIN

Life has a way of throwing curveballs that definitely test our swing. Only you can determine what your response will be to life's curveballs. Curveballs can be the final straws that break us, or the wedge that creates space for better things to emerge. When we experience multiple curveballs it gives us the practice that we need in order to correct our swing and perform better during our next time at bat. Despite what happens, you must keep your eye on the ball, take your swings, and maintain a healthy sense of optimism that you're going to connect on every pitch. You may strike out a few times, but if you keep swinging, sooner or later you'll knock one out of the park!

I must admit that I'm a bit of an over achiever with a tenacious drive when it comes to certain things. As a child, I was notoriously precocious and always worked angles to set myself up for the best possible outcome in any situation—especially if it involved my older brother and sisters. In our home, it was truly survival of the fittest. Being the fourth of five children in a single family household during the Reagan era was economically good for Wall Street, but there was definitely no surplus at 225 Broughton Street. As a teenager, my idea of an economic plan was running my own barbershop from home, mowing lawns in the community, or working all day in farmers' fields.

Early one muggy summer morning when I was about eleven years old, my friend told me there was going to be a drawing to win a Nintendo game console at the local Aden's Mini Market in town. I desperately wanted that new system. So, without hesitation, we jumped on our rickety bicycles and raced into town at lightning speed. When I got to the store, I went inside and filled out a single entry slip with all of my info and placed it in the big white entry box.

When we started on our return trip home, I remembered that my friend was the Tom Brokaw of the neighborhood. If he told more kids the news about the drawing, the pool would grow and decrease my chances of winning. I needed to craft a winning strategy, not just for myself, but for all the kids in the neighborhood that would come over to play my new video game if I won.

We had made it halfway home when I told my friend to keep going, that I would catch up with him later. I circled around and went back to the store with the intention of filling out another entry slip. When I made it back to the store, I found that according to the rules there was no limit to the number of forms I could submit. I'd found a legitimate loop hole and capitalized on it. I stayed for about an hour and filled out as many slips as I could. I stood outside and filled them out until I started getting cramps in my hand from writing. I filled the box until it spilled over with entries. I must have submitted over one hundred entry slips!

I went home and a few hours later my friend ran up to my doorstep screaming, "You won! You won!" At first I wondered how he'd gotten the word so soon. Then he told me, not only did I win a Nintendo, but I won every prize the store had up for grabs during that drawing. I raced back to the store. It was Christmas in the summer! Now, the toughest part was trying to lug that cumbersome Nintendo box (and my other prizes) all the way home on the push scooter that I also won, while holding on to one handle bar. From this experience I learned that extreme success follows extreme efforts!

To shift your life's momentum you must be proactive, and when required, be willing to test limits and go the extra mile. When you spot a great opportunity, exploit it without being unprincipled. To put it another way, be strategic versus being opportunistic. Being strategic means that you've viewed and thought through all sides of a problem. It's a process of figuring out what works and what doesn't by looking at what others have tried. It means formulating an executable plan within the rules of the game that will give you a strategic advantage.

In order to win at life, sometimes you will have to do things that others aren't willing to do. Some days will require you to stretch yourself to perform outside of your range. You must be agile and prepared to burn the midnight oil. When others are sleeping in, you'll have to get up early. When others aren't willing to continue learning, you'll have to keep your head in the books. When others aren't willing to invest the energy, you'll have to ask God for strength and stamina to keep going. There will be moments when you just have to keep filling out those slips of paper or plug away at the grunt work. In most cases you will have to endure hand cramps and chip away at your goals all by yourself!

EXPECT GREATNESS

As I conducted research for his book, I came across various academic theories regarding laws of expectation that were associated with the new age metaphysics. Its central premise held that whatever one expects with full confidence becomes a self-fulfilling prophecy. I do not draw my focus from any branch of metaphysics or unbiblical forms of universal law; however, I do extract the full wealth of my conclusions from key principles outlined in God's law—the Bible.

One may argue that glaring similarities exist between the principles that I'm sharing and other philosophical concepts, but the fundamental difference is revealed through who my hope and expectation is anchored in—the God of hope. The scriptures encourage us to look toward the God of hope who fills us with joy and peace. The apostle Paul's letter to the Romans states it this way, "Now the God of hope fill you with all joy and peace in believing, that ye may abound in hope."[11] Paul is saying that God is the sole source of expectation and will never fail us. We can anticipate great and miraculous things from him because he'll always abundantly exceed our expectations.

As people of faith, our expectations should be compatible with God's design for our lives. Let's examine this in context. The scriptures state, "For I know the plans I have for you," declares the LORD, "plans to prosper you and not to harm you, plans to give you hope and a future." (Jeremiah 29:11 NIV) This particular passage explains that with sovereign discipline, our Creator has drafted a blueprint for our lives that is engineered for positive outcomes. He has deliberately set our future to be jam-packed with success, security, and opportunities. If this is the plan that God has crafted for our lives, why do we develop lifelong insecurities from past failures and over burden ourselves with worry about our future?

Life happens! There will be days when you'll be disappointed. Once we overcome a traumatic experience it does not automatically rid us of the thought or anxiety we felt at the time we were going through the experience. It's completely okay to feel that way, but how will you move past it and rebuild healthy expectations? During these instances we must allow the Holy Spirit (God) to reprogram and guide our thoughts and actions. Through his guidance, we'll learn how to manage our expectations when we face similar situations in the future and not become devastated when things spin out of control.

Have you ever heard these statements? "Don't get your hopes up" or "Hope for the best, but expect the worst." Why not "Hope for the best and readjust during the worst"? Readjusting expectations does not mean you should lower your standards and become pessimistic. It simply means you should modify your outlook to be more compatible with the situation you are currently dealing with. The way you perceive things can be a game changer. You must move beyond adaptability to searching for the good, recognizing what is good, and then build strategies that will work out for your good even when bad things happen. In other words, you must widen your aperture to see things differently.

For example, the premise behind optometry is to identify defects in natural vision that hinder a person's quality of life. Before medical advancements such as LASIK and PRK, optometrists adjusted and corrected optical discrepancies with prescription eyeglasses or contact lenses. This type of prescription eyewear did not address the internal factors that contributed to a patient's poor vision, but they did correct how a patient with poor vision saw things. In other words, there will be times when you may never understand why bad things happen, but when you view life through different lenses you'll gain clarity and better understand how to readjust when they do.

Life is not about ignoring or refusing to see things that are awry. It is about nourishing yourself with optimism to view wrong things from the right perspective. It is about accepting wider parameters. If our expectations fall within too narrow boundaries, the likelihood that we will be disappointed goes way up.

OPTIMISTIC ATTITUDES PUT US IN CONTROL

Everyone wants to know how to live a better life. Here's a secret—you must be a positive thinker. Did you know that your life is continually being shaped by the expectations that you develop concerning your future? It is hard to believe that something as simple as setting positive expectations every day can benefit us in so many ways. I realize there may be other factors that influence the life you are leading. By no means am I suggesting that you should live with your head in the clouds, believing that you will be exempt from experiencing difficulties. I *am* suggesting that being optimistic helps clear the path to see the silver lining.

Optimists have a natural tendency to believe and expect the best outcome. The word *optimism* comes from the Latin word *optimus*, which means "best."[12] From a doctrinal standpoint, it means the world is the "best of all possible worlds" in which the Creator accomplishes the most good at the cost of the least evil. Understanding the root meaning of this word helps us better appreciate why an optimistic person always searches for the greatest amount of good in any situation, despite the position they may be in.

Let me share a personal experience with you. I often think about when I applied to become a commissioned officer in the United States Air Force. I was an enlisted Staff Sergeant and had graduated from college at the top of my class. It was tough balancing the demands of my job, a new family, and deployments, but I still managed to perform at extremely high levels and earned numerous annual awards for my work.

One night after an annual awards ceremony, several people asked me if I had ever considered submitting an application for Officer Training School (OTS). I had toyed with the idea early in my career, but my passion for it quickly fizzled and died because of negativity from my peers and others. I bought into their rhetoric instead of creating my own reality.

A few years had passed, my perspective changed, and I matured beyond other people's opinions. I was finally ready to give OTS a shot. My wife and I prayed together about it and I started working on my application. I had the full support of my squadron commander and a few others. However, my shop chief at the time told me that he had applied for OTS twice and was denied—even with a master's degree! He told me not to count on being selected, especially with such low Air Force Officer Qualifying Test scores and the extremely low selection rates that year. Even though my chances were slim to none, I had different expectations—I expected to become an Air Force officer.

As I carried my application from office to office to get the required endorsements before mailing it off, I found a note (that I should not have seen) buried inside my application folder. It was written from my Maintenance Group Chief Master Sergeant to my Maintenance Group Colonel. Despite my numerous awards and being ranked as the number one technician in the Maintenance Group, he seriously questioned whether or not I was officer material. It also said that "If performance records are the basis for selection, he is climbing a steep hill." I was a bit discouraged and confused, but it fueled my drive to succeed—I expected to become an officer. This wasn't the first time I had experienced negativity in my career and I was certain that it wouldn't be my last. I finally finished my application and sent it in. The results were to be released a few months later.

My education counselor told me that if I was selected for OTS I would get a call from him at 0900 hours (9:00 a.m.) on the day of the news release. Needless to say, at 0900 hours, I did not receive the phone call. I was terribly disappointed but remained optimistic that better things were up ahead for me. I had worked hard and knew it was a long shot, but I was content, because I had given it my best. I remained quietly focused for most of the day, but kept my head up and starting building new strategies for my next move.

At about 1500 hours (3:00 p.m.) I began cleaning up my work station and was preparing to go home for the day. I started thinking about how I would share the news with my wife. I started toward the restroom to wash my hands when I received a page over the loud-speaker that I had a phone call in the office.

I answered the phone; it was my shop chief. He paused and then released a heavy sigh before saying anything. In my mind, I just knew he was going to rub in the fact that I was not selected for OTS. He told me that our commander wanted to see me. I asked him if he knew why. Then he said, "Congratulations, you made it." I was shocked. I said, "Are you serious?" He said, "Please be at the base theater at 1600 hours." When I arrived at the theater, my entire squadron was there to congratulate me. They had secretly held the news from me for an entire day. A few weeks later I was off to OTS!

I learned that having an optimistic attitude can help us regain momentum and add thrust when things have stalled. Simply put, it can motivate us to lace up our track spikes and engage life with the mindset to hurdle every obstacle and win! When life presents us with opportunities we must use them to make forward progress without stagnating. We must put forth our best efforts and maintain a good attitude in all that we do. As we put in the effort to change and improve, we must be aware that things and people around us are also changing and improving. Despite any disadvantage we may feel we have, we must resolve to move forward and finish what we start.

Successful living begins when we learn to use positivity to our advantage. It is not always about our position, but rather our disposition. Maintaining positive attitudes and expectations gives us the upper hand as we navigate our way through the uncertainties of life. Those expectations serve to buoy our assumptions that something positive will happen, often in contrast to our current reality. They are an intense hope where we envision favorable outcomes in our future. They position us to experience peace during chaos—the type of peace that comes only after we've done our part and expected God to manage the outcome! We must continuously strive to shift our attitudes and perceptions. Attitude determines altitude.

Our attitudes are an essential factor to achieving 100 percent success. Brian Tracy once stated, "You cannot control what happens to you, but you can control your attitude toward what happens to you, and in that, you will be mastering change rather than allowing it to master you." It is important to gain a clear perspective on life and understand the things that will ensure our success. Here is a simple formula of what makes our lives 100 percent successful.[13]

If

A B C D E F G H I J K L M N O P Q R S T U V W X Y Z

Is equal to

1 2 3 4 5 6 7 8 9 10 11 12 13 14 15 16 17 18 19 20 21 22 23 24 25 26

Hard Work

H+A+R+D+W+O+R+K

$8+1+18+4+23+15+18+11 =$ **98%**

Knowledge

K+N+O+W+L+E+D+G+E

$11+14+15+23+12+5+4+7+5 =$ **96%**

Love

L+O+V+E

$12+15+22+5 =$ **54%**

Luck

L+U+C+K

$12+21+3+11 =$ **47%**

Is it money that makes life 100%?

Money

M+O+N+E+Y

13+15+14+5+25 = **72%**

What about Leadership?

Leadership

L+E+A+D+E+R+S+H+I+P

12+5+1+4+5+18+19+9+16 = **89%**

What is it that makes life 100%? Every problem has a solution, but to go to the top and achieve 100%, we must go a little further

Attitude

A+T+T+I+T+U+D+E

1+20+20+9+20+21+4+5 = **100%**

It is our attitude towards life and work that makes our life = 100%

Persist Until Success Happens
Life Application Exercise

1.   Disregard toxic words and ignore what negative people say or think about you.

2.   Use positive words and practice encouraging self-talk throughout the day.

3.   See the good in every situation...think positively. It might take some time for the changes to take place, but eventually they will.

SMALL STEPS TOWARD BIG SUCCESS

Optimism puts you in control: Have a positive outlook on life. Bring positive energy and infuse motivating self-talk into your daily routine. You'll be more productive when you adopt a positive outlook over a negative one. Face challenges head on and look for the silver lining in all situations.

CHAPTER 6

SEE IT!

What you see is what you get!

A critical element for achieving success in life comes from your ability to create a strong mental picture or vision for your future. Habakkuk 2:2 reads "And the LORD answered me, and said, write the vision, and make [it] plain upon tables, that he may run that readeth it." In other words, write what you see. Write it in big block letters so that it can be read on the run!"[14] Whether you're sixteen or sixty, it's never too late write a vision for your life.

When I speak of vision, I am not defining it in terms of physically viewing things with your eyes, but how you see things happening in your future through the eye of your mind. It's your ability to perceive positive outcomes before they occur. Vision is created when you begin to transform your ideas into imagery in your mind. Vision is when you challenge the status quo and breach the outer parameters of thought to act on the dreams inside your head. People who possess vision can tap into spiritual power to change the environment around them. They can see beyond current limitations to accomplish their goals. They always excel at the level in which they dream. Take the Tuskegee Airmen for instance.

Imagine fighting and dying to defend your country, a country that initially said that, because of your racial origin you possessed neither the brains nor the intelligence to operate such a complicated weapon system as an aircraft. Throughout World War II there were many African American pilots who served with distinction in the United States Army Air Corps.[15] These pilots unselfishly gave their lives for their country, yet they were forgotten. This fighting group of individuals made a major impact in the war through their superb piloting skills. Despite their success, the African American pilots were never given the respect they deserved from their own nation, a nation that was severely prejudiced. Almost fifty years after the war, those dedicated servicemen finally received the recognition they so richly deserved. These men are known today as the Tuskegee Airmen. These mighty men of vision and valor proved they had what it took, not only in war, but also in peacetime. They were pioneers who paved the way by overcoming countless obstacles to become the most successful leaders of their time. Airmen such as General Benjamin Davis endured four years of "silent treatment" from his classmates at West Point; but he endeavored to persevere and went on to become the first black general in the Air Force and form and shape the prestigious Tuskegee Airmen.

When I taught at Air University at Maxwell Air Force Base in Montgomery, Alabama I had the opportunity to share some very memorable moments with Lieutenant Colonel (Lt Col) Herbert Carter who was one of the original members of the Tuskegee Airmen. Lt Col Carter was an outstanding fighter pilot who flew seventy-seven bomber aircraft escort missions through very direct and intense anti-aircraft fire over Europe during World War II. Each semester our staff would invite Lt Col Carter to share his experiences with our students. He was well into his nineties and was confined to a wheelchair. By then his body was very limited but his mind was extremely sharp. During his visits I would escort him to center stage in front of the massive crowd of students. He would sit in his wheelchair with debonair poise and timeless wisdom and recount his flying days with vivid detail. He told stories about the challenges of integration and how the black man was labeled as lazy, lackadaisical, and had neither the physiological nor psychological qualities necessary for leadership. He told us how he was able to overcome hardships and the grim realities of serving in a racially divided armed service. Times were tough for him; but he envisioned a better future for African American pilots, and he set out to dispel the myths of his critics. Those days would finally come when his unit, the 99th Fighter Squadron, and other squadrons of the 332nd Fighter Group compiled an outstanding record of performance in tactical air and ground support of Allied Armies, including destroying seventeen German aircraft over Anzio Beach during the Allied Forces invasion of Northern Italy.

The historical developments, primary roles, and accomplishments of the Tuskegee Airmen during World War II laid the foundation for African Americans and other races to join the Army Air Forces. These brave pilots proved they could be victorious in all our nation's conflicts, overseas and in their homeland. It is important that we, as a nation, never forget the sacrifices and efforts of these dedicated men. They helped us to better comprehend their lives as African Americans during World War II. Facing segregation and blatant racism daily, they adapted, overcame, and excelled. We as a nation are indeed indebted to each of these men. These men were, and still are, our nation's finest visionaries and unsung heroes and should never be forgotten.

If we survey the Tuskegee Airmen, we find that they all had the ability to see success and they acted on their vision without fear. As a result, they lived out their vision, excelled, and accomplished their dreams.

There is a sobering reality experienced by many people when they fail to create a vision for themselves. Proverbs 29:18 reads, "Where there is no vision, the people perish." In simple terms, lack of vision kills your future and robs you of your destiny. If you can't see a clear mental image of things happening for you, then you may never feel inspired to try to accomplish greater things in life, and you'll continue to retreat to complacency and fear. When this happens, the only thing people will remember about you is your legacy of underachievement.

It is time to envision yourself winning, achieving, and accomplishing your dreams despite the obstacles you may be facing. You must see success happening before it actually occurs by establishing a strong vision. Take a moment to write down everything you would like to accomplish in the upcoming days, weeks, months, and years. Be consistent in working toward your goals, track your progress, and before you know it your fantasies will become reality—but it all begins with developing a vision for your life.

Persist Until Success Happens
Life Application Exercise

Develop a Vision Board:

1. Reflect on the goals that you completed and those that you did not complete last year. Be grateful for your successes and failures. Decide whether or not you still want to continue pursuing the goals that you did not complete last year. Regret and negativity can kill your drive. In either case, remain positive.

2. Think about ten goals that you desire to complete this year. Find bold, inspiring pictures, words, and images on the Internet that best represent your current state, transition phase, and future state. Print them out. Write out the following headings on your corkboard: CURRENT STATE, TRANSITION PHASE, FUTURE STATE and year for completion. Place the corresponding photos under headings.

3. Now use your strategy map to think about where you desire to go and how you're going to get there this year. Each time you complete a goal, put a gold star on the photo. It may seem juvenile at first but trust me, it helps you identify milestones and visually track your progress in a motivational way! It also helps you to keep track of your blessings.

SMALL STEPS TOWARD BIG SUCCESS

Exude confidence and courage: To thrive in life you must be able to face life's giants head-on believing that you will win! There are times when we all feel inadequate or incapable for one reason or another. But in order to be successful, you have to be secure in your abilities and confident that you can complete any goal or task that is set before you. Never allow or tolerate anyone who makes you feel insignificant. Believe that God has given you the power to do all things through his strength.

CHAPTER 7

FIVE OR TEN YEARS FROM NOW

The best way to predict your future is to create it.
Abraham Lincoln

As you've scrolled through pictures in your social media accounts or thumbed through old photo albums, have you ever wondered "Where has the time gone?" The older you get, the faster time seems to pass. The rhetoric of our current culture suggests that thirty is the new twenty, forty is the new thirty and so on, but there are few things that help us prepare for these transformative periods in our lives. Without warning, and out of nowhere, you might begin to notice small armies of gray hair sprouting up and advancing into (or retreating from) previously occupied territory. You might not be as motivated as you were just a few years ago, and you may feel as if time is working against you. There is no need to panic...just keep calm and carry on. Aging happens to everyone who is fortunate enough to live a longer life! We all age, but not everyone matures.

I think of maturity as a self-governing mind-set encoded within us that helps us reach full development in terms of emotional, spiritual, and social behavior. God gave us this feature to keep us from living in an irresponsible and harmful manner. It is something that can be worked on and improved over time. Some people mature early in life, while others mature later or not at all. This is important because maturity is a key factor that undergirds our success and helps us remain under control throughout life. There are a few signs that point toward whether or not a person has matured in terms of emotional, spiritual, social, and financial behavior. Below is a short list of seven indicators you can use to assess your level of maturity.[16] As you review this list, don't be discouraged if you realize that you need to improve in certain areas. We all have weaknesses, strengths and extenuating circumstances. You should use this information as a tool to learn, grow, change, get help, and become a better version yourself.

Seven Indicators of Immaturity

1. *Impulsive, overindulgent, and lack self-control.* Whether it's over-eating, over spending, excessively entertaining yourself, obsessions with certain things, or your constant fixation with your phone and social media accounts, these are signs that point to an inability to control your desires and productively use your time.

2. *Reached mid-life and still live with parents or are overly reliant on them.* This does not include people who are providing care for elderly parents, have some type of debilitating disease, physical or mental limitations, or those who suddenly lost their job. Of course there may be other examples, but I'm sure you get my point. If you're healthy and able bodied you should leave the

nest and not burden your parents with your responsibilities and issues.

3. *Financially irresponsible.* This includes not being able to pay your monthly bills on time or without assistance from friends, relatives, co-workers, church, etc. This also means over spending, never budgeting, and racking up tons of unnecessary debt that you cannot replay due to poor decision-making.

4. *Have trouble keeping a job for more than a few months.* If you are chronically unemployed and never stay on a job more than a few months, this can be a sign of laziness, boredom, that you haven't found your niche, or may indicate issues with submitting to authority. Everyone needs a job and should be able to support themselves. Any job will do. Simply start somewhere and remain there until you build a good strategy for moving on to something that aligns with your goals. If you do not have a job, find one so you can build a good history of work experience. Then commit yourself to showing up on time, respecting others, and earning your pay.

5. *Have trouble building good lasting relationships.* You are unable to develop good healthy long-term relationships with people. You've never learned how to manage conflicts, overcome differences, and push through problems. Your default response is to put up guards, end the relationship, or start a new one. Your life becomes filled with failure in the area of commitment, respect, cooperation, and trust.

6. *Highly Emotional.* You have unchecked emotions and become easily offended when challenged or given feedback. During arguments you are always right and you often play the victim.

You never own your mistakes. You also tend to speak negatively of other people and are plagued by jealousy and insecurity. You are consistently jealous of other people's possessions, salaries, houses, cars, friends, physical appearance, or family. Can you celebrate the blessings of God in others' lives? Or does God's goodness to others stir up envy toward them in your heart?

7. *Never finish what you start.* Finishing what you start says a lot about your character. In life we must commit to doing things and see them through until the end. When you do not complete what you start it indicates that the task at hand is not very important to you and that you may be unreliable, unorganized, or unfocused.

Like a fine wine, we should get better as we age, but sometimes we fall short of becoming our best because of how we set our expectations during certain phases of our lives. We can be too hard on ourselves after we fail to reach certain goals. This can cause us to develop regrets, especially after we've repeatedly made unwise decisions throughout the course of our lives. On the other hand, maybe you're a young person with a clean slate who is full of big ideas and desire to do something ambitious and meaningful but don't know where to start. Because of your desire to get the ball rolling you might make a few hasty moves and start down a path that is not right for you. In either scenario, because of our sensitivity to time we often force ourselves into doing things that we're not passionate about instead of finding a path that allows us to naturally flow in the areas we enjoy and can succeed. As a mentor and advisor, I see it all the time. Many people I interact with spend thousands of dollars pursuing college degrees in fields they are not passionate about in order to do a job for forty hours a week that they hate. After several years of being in the trenches, some people become so emotionally drained that it begins to take a vicious toll on their health and causes them to spiral into midlife crisis.

KEEP CALM IT'S ONLY A MID-LIFE CRISIS

Midlife crisis is a term first coined by Elliott Jaques referring to a critical phase in a person›s life during their forties to early sixties based on periods of transition.[17] Most people imagine a mid-life crisis as a middle-aged hairy-chested man in an open collared shirt naughtily flirting with an uninterested young lady from the window of his brand new Porsche 911. Not every midlife crisis manifests in this way. Sometimes a mid-life crisis can manifest in a much milder manner as we compare our dreams against our current reality. For example, you may have worked hard throughout the years and made decent earnings, but never earned that top promotion you desired. You might have been working toward developing a great investment portfolio or building a nice nest egg for retirement, but now you have little to show for it because of unforeseen life circumstances. You may even have envisioned owning a nice home or a small business, but things never quite materialized for you because of major setbacks. Trust me, life can be a roller coaster ride of twists and turns, ups and downs that cause you to experience drastic drops in your stomach as you freefall into unexpected situations. This causes many people to see their lives as unsuccessful, which puts them in perpetual crisis management mode instead of in crisis planning mode. It is during these times that we wish we could have had some type of forewarning of things to come, or knew some way to design or plan certainty into our lives. As you reflect further on your life, you might even wish you could turn back the hands of time and do some things differently. If life had an undo button, what decisions would you reverse? If you had superpowers and could take a quantum leap into your future, what advice would you bring back and tell yourself today? How would you plan your future?

With those questions in mind, where do you see yourself five or ten years from now? What do you plan to achieve? Do you envision yourself winning and being highly productive while enjoying a posh lifestyle in bourgeois suburbia? Do you imagine the next five to ten years to be spiritually, physically, emotionally, and financially rewarding? Or do you think it's too late to experience a great life? In the words of Abraham Lincoln, "The best way to predict your future is to create it." We all have the power to create the lives we desire, but we must see the future version of ourselves and focus our efforts toward becoming that version. Life is too short to continue looking at it through a rear view mirror. Our drive, energy, and focus must be directed toward completing daily goals and advancing toward future prospects. If you desire to live a successful life, you must be intentional about the things you do today and become more strategic regarding decisions that affect your success in the future.

YOU'RE NOT A LONG SHOT

Sometimes we make misguided choices in life because we do not listen to what data tells us. Let me add more context to my statement as we take a look at some numbers. A 2013 Rasmussen Reports[18] survey of one thousand people revealed that 88 percent of Americans believed that individuals made their own success in the United States. According to the study, 88 percent of American adults thought it was at least "somewhat likely" that anyone who worked hard and made good decisions would enjoy a middle-class lifestyle, including 38 percent of that number who said it was "very likely." Only 10 percent of respondents believed it was "not very" or "not at all likely" to achieve a middleclass lifestyle through hard work.

The results provided a fascinating look into how many Americans view success. All things considered, there appears to be a consensus among many Americans that you can have the life you desire if you're willing to put in the work and make wise decisions. Take a moment to consider where you stand within the survey. Are you among the 88 percent majority that sees lifetime success as an achievable outcome, or are you in the 10 percent minority that views it as being unlikely?

There are numerous factors that influence how people view success. Sometimes our views of success can be influenced through factors such as gender, age, and culture. A poll conducted for Time and Real Simple revealed that for most women, the concept of success constantly changed as they aged. For example, young women tended to be more ambitious, with 73 percent saying it was "very important" for them to be successful at work, compared to 37 percent of women in their '60s. Given the previous definitions and numbers, it is apparent that success means different things to different people. We should each determine our own definition of success and exert the required amount of energy and effort toward that end state. Don't allow yourself to be pulled into the small segment of society that harbors negative views about life due to the setbacks they've experienced. Misery loves company, but you don't have to accept the invitation to anyone's pity party. Trust me, there are a lot of miserable folks in the world, but you do not have to be one of them. You can experience the true joy and happiness that results from finding your purpose in life and being plugged into a great network of supportive people to push you toward greater success. At the risk of being redundant, let me say it again, you have the power to choose what you want your life to become but you must keep pushing.

Chances are, like many people you may not fully know what you want to do with your life—even after finishing school or landing a good paying job. It's not unusual to feel this way. That's because many of us haven't identified our purpose or niche in life. It gets even more complicated as we age. We avoid taking on new ventures because we feel that we don't have enough time, or because it makes us vulnerable to embarrassment if we fail. As a result, we spend most of our lives fantasizing about doing great things but never take action on them.

Everything in life begins with making a decision, and you must choose whether you're going to walk by faith or tiptoe in fear. The apostle Paul wrote, "We walk by faith, not by sight."[19] In other words, our sight allows us to gain knowledge of the visible world and that knowledge provides insight to where we should go. Walking by faith, however, works differently. It requires that we walk into unfamiliar territory with limited knowledge, allowing our beliefs to guide us in the right direction. Living by faith means that we step out before we know how things are going to turn out. In other words, you must have an irrational sense of optimism that things are going to work out—even when the odds are against you and the path is unclear. You're not a long shot, with God you're a sure shot. You must believe that all things will work together for your good.

Living by faith means that you maintain a clear perspective concerning what you desire from life. It causes you to get excited about your prospects, pursuits, and dreams. Your excitement will keep you encouraged and enable you to gain momentum in your quest for success. As you adjust your behaviors and channel your efforts, you will soon begin to view your life with more precision. You'll begin to understand where you fit in the world and how to make greater contributions to it. When your perception about life changes—so will your reality. Don't procrastinate for another five or ten years until you think everything will be perfect. Things will never be perfect and your timing will not always be perfect. Make a move toward your dreams today! It all begins with writing down a list of goals and creating a life strategy to achieve them. When you take the first step and write out a list of goals it moves you to the top 3 percent of adults in our society, yes that's right, 97 percent of adults have never written out a list of goals they'd like to achieve in their lifetime.[20] This is shocking, but true. Are you ready to join the top 3 percent of goal oriented adults in society? There is a spot at the top reserved for you, but you must work for it.

Let's take a few moments to begin laying the foundation for building your life strategy. This requires you to take a personal assessment of where you are now, what you'd like to improve, and where you desire to be in the future. Take a moment to honestly write down answers to the following questions on the PUSH page.

Persist **U**ntil **S**uccess **H**appens
Life Application Exercise

1. **Where do you want to be in five or ten years from now?**

2. **Take inventory and assess what is going on in your life.** Briefly write down what is going on in your current situation. Consider your spiritual life, your relationships with others, your job, your health (physical and emotional), your finances, etc.

3. **How would you currently rate or score your life?** How would you score your life in terms of the success you've experienced? Are you extremely satisfied, satisfied, somewhat satisfied, not at all satisfied? Write down your answer.

4. **What are your faucets?** Write down the things that you enjoy doing and the areas where you thrive. In other words, what causes rivers of happiness, joy, and satisfaction to flow in your life? What are your greatest accomplishments? What makes you laugh? What inspires you?

5. **What are your drains?** Identify and jot down the things that drain positive energy from your life? Determine who, what, when, why, and where the toxic areas are in your life. What people, decisions, behaviors, habits, or situations cause you worry, anxiety, and stress?

6. **What things are not working in your life?** Identify and write down the dysfunctional areas in your life that cause you to be unhappy and slightly depressed. What things are out of sync and lack balance? What challenges and struggles do you face

daily? What are you dissatisfied with? What are your shortcomings, weaknesses, and failures?

7. **What do you envision your life becoming?** Write down your answers to the following questions: If there were absolutely no limits to what you could have, do, or become in life, what would you choose to do or be? Where do you want to go? How do you desire to live? How do you want to feel?

Review the answers to your questions and take a moment to think about your life in the near term and in the future. The answers you provided will help identify target areas for improvement and give you goals to PUSH toward.

SMALL STEPS TOWARD BIG SUCCESS

Seek continuous improvement: Each day you should strive to be better than you were the day before. If you attempt to overhaul your life in one day, it will not last! We need to make consistent improvements and gradual changes that can be sustained over time. Incorporating new habits in your daily routine can have a dramatic effect on your level of success. Don't be afraid to step out on faith and take risks and make mistakes. Life is about learning, growth, and optimization.

CHAPTER 8

DESIGN YOUR SUCCESS

Success is not the key to happiness. Happiness is the key to
success. If you love what you are doing, you will be successful.
-Albert Schweitzer

WHAT IS SUCCESS?

In some circles, success is defined as the result of getting or achieving wealth, respect, or fame.[21] This definition is somewhat contracted and is screaming to be expanded in so many ways. I've asked countless people around the world to share their views of what success meant to them. Many people saw success as living their lives the way they truly desired and deserved. Some viewed it as power, prestige, achievement of personal goals, or pleasure; while others viewed it as the happiness derived from being connected and full in their relationship with God, their families, and friends. Several viewed success as the achievement of an action in a specified amount of time, while others defined it as the peace of mind that comes from knowing they gave their best effort toward a goal. In short, one's view of success is largely dependent on the context of what a person thinks is important in life.

From a spiritual perspective, I believe that success is progressive. It is a gradual release of God's wisdom to accomplish his work through our lives with the ultimate aim of helping others. When his will is accomplished, it has an eternal value in this world and the world to come. In my opinion, success comes as a result of developing the right habits to properly manage and preserve our most critical resources: our spirits, health, time, money, and relationships. It occurs as we cultivate the right behaviors internally and allow him to take care of the results externally. This calls us to greater heights of stewardship and responsibility over the gifts and opportunities we are given in life. It also helps us ground our motives in morality and serve the greater good.

While the interpretation of success may vary from person to person, the principles remain the same. No matter how old you are, where you are from, or what you do for a living, we all share this in common—we desire to experience the greatest success that God has to offer! It is important for those of us who are Christians to remember that God wants us to be successful. The scriptures state that if we commit our actions to the LORD, our plans will succeed.[22] However, we should never compromise our relationship with him by focusing all our attention on achieving success. Our focus should be on pleasing him and doing his will. As you continue this journey through the remaining chapters of this book, take a moment to ask yourself these questions: Why is being successful important to me? What do I stand to lose if I don't pursue my goals? Am I chasing after success with the wrong motives? Is success worth fighting for?

BUILDING STRATEGIES

Good strategies create windows for us to see the possibilities and opportunities that exist in every situation. They also prevent us from chasing our dreams in a reckless manner because they arm us with the appropriate knowledge we need to run after them intelligently. In other words, strategies provide a rational framework to set goals and point us toward the ideal way to achieve them. They enable us to recognize the border between what is possible and what is impossible and help us chart the best way forward from that notion. They help us engineer a better way to live.

Some of you may be wondering if strategic planning is a biblical concept. Proverbs 19:21 declares, "Many are the plans in a man's heart, but it is the Lord's purpose that prevails."[23] Without question, it is God's plan we want, not our own. From this verse we can conclude that God's purpose should be the centerpiece of the strategic planning process. We must involve him from the outset of our endeavors. We should not trust our own plans and strategies and completely ignore the guidance of the Holy Spirit. When we seek the heart of God and his direction, we can establish plans that are pleasing to him, and have confidence that those plans will succeed. By principle and by example, God's Word establishes strategic planning as one of the ways he works in and through his people.[24] Let's look at a few biblical examples such as Moses and King David.

When God called Moses to lead the children of Israel out of bondage from Egypt it was a remarkable assignment. Moses learned to appreciate the concept of strategic thinking when he was charged with the care, feeding, and logistical movement of thousands of people out of bondage from Egypt. Moses' father-in-law Jethro noticed that Moses was having a difficult time bearing the burden of leading a nation. With great wisdom, Jethro taught Moses how to set up a strategic plan by delegating management and oversight to different officers and by spreading the workload among the people. As a result, the manpower resources were used more effectively and ministry was accomplished. Moses was also thinking strategically when he sent spies to gather intelligence in the land of Canaan.

We also find that David was a skilled warrior who used strategic thinking from his youth to kill lions, bears, and the Philistine giant Goliath. He knew how to fight with accuracy and precision when he defeated Goliath using a God-given strategy that exploited the vulnerabilities of his enemy.[25] David also used strategic planning to set his army in array during battle. He also selected warriors who could think and plan strategically and won many battles over the Philistines and Moabites, just to name a few. They made plans, so they could properly respond to challenges by being proactive instead of reactive. This is why it is important for us to plan ahead, so we can identify the associated risks, weigh and categorize them, prioritize and create a flexible response plan and not merely play things by ear.

Many people know what they'd like to do in order to be successful, but few build strategies to help them get there. In order for us to build an effective strategy, first we'll need to understand and define what a strategy is. The word *strategy* is indirectly derived from the Greek word *strategos* meaning "generalship." The Greek equivalent for the modern word *strategy* would have been *strategike episteme* (general's knowledge) or *strategon sophia* (general's wisdom).[26] Like a military officer, strategies provide wisdom and overall direction for completing objectives. Such was the case with King David and his armies. A strategy is the ends, ways, and means by which one accomplishes an overall goal. It is the deliberate actions one takes and the instruments one uses to reach a desired outcome. It is a system that can be used to predict and ensure continuous success. Early in my military career as an Air Force officer, it was made abundantly clear that I had to learn to think strategically and develop plans to guide our squadron's efforts. Without solid strategies it would have been extremely difficult for our organization to achieve its mission and goals.

Strategies are important because they establish a structure for getting things done. They outline your vision, mission, and the end state you intend to achieve. They suggest the paths you should take and the best ways to advance forward. Good strategies tend to factor in barriers, resources, and they exploit key windows of opportunity. To build effective strategies you must be flexible, adaptable, and able to anticipate the things that are going to happen. You must ask questions, brainstorm, and jot down relevant ideas to facilitate your desired end state. This is called strategic thinking.

STRATEGIC THINKING

Strategic thinking requires great foresight, vision, and understanding of how to solve problems. It's critically thinking of ways to succeed in a manner that puts you out in front of the curve. Strategic thinking enables you to see the bigger picture and broader perspective concerning your overall goals. There are several things that strategic thinkers do very well:

1. **They can anticipate** what can happen next and adapt to the situation before it occurs. It is similar to predicting your opponent's next few moves when playing chess or checkers. Strategic thinkers make predictions based on what they know and make assumptions about things they do not know. They create short, medium, and long range planning cycles. Strategic thinkers are often able to get out in front of potential problems while positioning themselves to gain an advantage.

2. **They're innovative and imaginative.** They think of creative and often unconventional ways to solve problems. They are not confined to the parameters of status quo thinking. They are non-judgmental when presented with new ideas and information.

3. **They develop habits of mind.** Habits of mind are outlooks that are skillfully and mindfully employed by intelligent, successful people when they are confronted with problems. In their book, *Habits of Mind: A Developmental Series*, authors Arthur L. Costa and Bena Kallick define habits of mind as the following sixteen attributes that intelligent human beings do when they are solving problems.[27] This list is not all inclusive:

    - **Persisting**-Sticking to a task until it is completed.
    - **Managing Impulsivity**-Thinking before one acts.
    - **Listening with Understanding and Empathy**-Attending to another person and demonstrating an understanding of and empathy for an idea or feeling.
    - **Thinking about Thinking (Metacognition)**-Metacognition is the ability to know what we know and what we don't know. It's also the ability to plan a strategy for producing what information is needed, to be conscious of our own steps and strategies during the act of problem solving, and to reflect on and evaluate the productiveness of our own thinking.
    - **Striving for Accuracy**- The desire for craftsmanship, mastery, flawlessness, and economy of energy to produce exceptional results.
    - **Thinking flexibly**- Having the ability to change one's mind while receiving additional input. The ability to consider alternative points of view or deal with several sources of information simultaneously. Flexible thinking is when one's mind is

open to change based on additional information and data or reasoning, which contradicts their beliefs.

- **Questioning and Posing Problems**-Effective problem solvers know how to ask questions to fill in the gaps with insight and intuition.
- **Applying Past Knowledge to New Situations**-When confronted with a new and perplexing problem they will often draw forth experience from their past.
- **Thinking and Communicating with Clarity and Precision**-When one avoids hasty overgeneralizations, deletions, and distortions and instead supports their statements with explanations, comparisons, quantification, and evidence.
- **Gathering Data through All Senses**-Using all of one's faculties to take in information.
- **Creating, Imagining, and Innovating**-Creative human beings try to conceive problem solutions differently and examin alternative possibilities from many angles. They tend to project themselves into different roles using analogies, by starting with a vision and working backward, or by imagining they are the objects being considered.
- **Responding with Wonderment and Awe**-Those creative thinkers who have a passion for what they do. Efficacious people have not only an "I can" attitude, but also an "I enjoy" feeling.
- **Taking Responsible Risks**-Thinkers who accept confusion, uncertainty, and the higher risks of failure as part of the normal process and learn to view setbacks as interesting, challenging, and growth producing. They do not, however, behave impulsively. Their risks are educated. They draw on past knowledge, are thoughtful about consequences, and have a well-trained sense of what is appropriate.

- **Finding Humor**-It has been found to liberate creativity and provoke such higher level thinking skills as anticipation, finding novel relationships, visual imagery, and making analogies.
- **Thinking Interdependently**-Cooperative humans realize that all of us thinking together are more powerful, intellectually and/or physically, than any one individual.
- **Remaining Open to Continuous Learning**-People with this Habit of Mind are always striving for improvement, always growing, always learning, always modifying and improving themselves. They seize problems, situations, tensions, conflicts and circumstances as valuable opportunities to learn.

4. **They use patterns of inquiry**. This means they gain knowledge from their past experiences and use that knowledge to question and challenge the problem at hand.

5. **They are lifelong learners**. They seek out knowledge that leads to continuous improvement.

6. **They are logical, rational, and reasonable**. They define their objectives and plan accordingly.

7. **They are emotionally intelligent.** They are amazingly aware and perceptive and understand how to effectively lead, influence, and interact with others.

GOAL SETTING

Goal setting is the best system for planning your ideal future state. It allows you to choose where you want to go in life. It helps you build your short and long-term strategies and helps shape your decision-making. It enables you to focus on the things that are important and helps you to organize your resources.

By setting precise, clearly defined goals, you can measure and take pride in the achievement of those goals. You can see forward progress in what might previously have seemed a long pointless grind. Also, setting goals helps raise your self-confidence as you begin to recognize your ability and competence in achieving the goals you have set. The process of achieving goals and seeing this achievement motivates you to soar to higher heights.

A practical way of making goals more powerful is to use the SMART mnemonic.[28] While there are plenty of variations (some of which are included in parenthesis), SMART usually stands for:

S– Specific (or Significant) Your goal should clearly state what, where, when, and how your goals are to be achieved. Sometimes it may even state why that goal is important.

M– Measurable (or Meaningful) It has been said that what cannot be measured cannot be managed. This is often true when it comes to goals. Sometimes it is difficult to measure a goal, but at such times there is usually an indirect measure that can be applied. This refers to both the end results and milestones along the way to attaining a goal. It answers the question of quantity – how much, how often and how many. The milestones are signs along the way that will tell you that you are on the right track to achieving your goal. For instance, your ultimate goal may be to earn 1,200 dollars in bonus money in a year, but the milestones may be to make 100 dollars every month, which will add up to 1,200 in a year. So by focusing on making the 100 dollars every month you will ultimately reach your goal of 1,200 dollars by the end of the year. This makes the goal more attainable because it is easier to think of ways to make 100 dollars in bonus every month rather than 1,200 all at once.

A– Attainable (or Action Oriented) You should ensure that the goals you set can be achieved. You must believe and have faith that all things are possible, but you must be realistic. If you set goals that are unbelievable even to yourself it is very unlikely you will achieve them. This is equally important when setting goals for a group, such as in a corporate setting.

R– Relevant (or Rewarding) Your goals must be relevant to what you want to achieve in the short and long term. Understanding your personal vision, mission, and purpose is critical in this respect. Sometimes you can be tempted to do something simply because it is easy and sounds great, only to discover later that it has no long term importance to what you want to achieve as an individual. Do those things that are most important and in line with your long term vision and mission.

T– Time-based (or Trackable) This sometimes overlaps with the goal being Specific, but it aims to ensure that you put a time-frame to your goals. Someone said a goal is a dream with a time-frame. Simply deciding when you want to achieve something by can be a good motivator. It can prevent you from procrastinating because you know you are working to a deadline. "Failing to plan is planning to fail" If you find yourself unable to set a SMART goal it is more than likely that your future plans are not clear enough and need to be worked on. Furthermore, do not be tempted to skip the process of SMART goal setting and "get on with it" without fully analyzing your goals. Doing this careful planning at the beginning will save you lots of time and disappointment at a later stage and you will avoid making costly mistakes.

A critical step in developing a good strategy is asking the right questions. It is the reason most plans fail. Here is a list, not all inclusive, of fundamental questions you should ask yourself when you're brainstorming questions to develop a strategy:

BRAINSTORMING

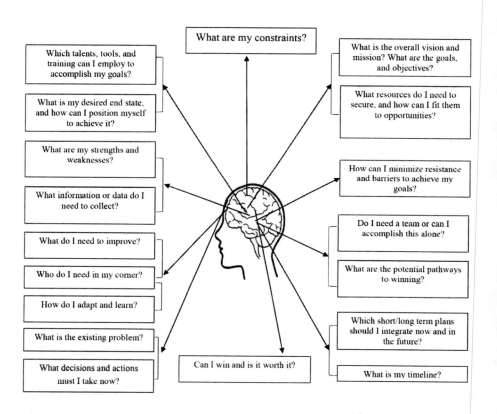

STRATEGIC PLAN

Once you've answered these questions, you'll be ready to start building your strategy on a dry erase board. The scriptures declare that, "The steps of a good man are ordered by the LORD."[29] This step-by-step model can be applied and modified to walk you through just about everything you want to do (provided you tweak it here and there). First let's establish the framework for your strategic plan. We'll break your plan down into three major areas moving progressively from left to right:

STRATEGY MAP

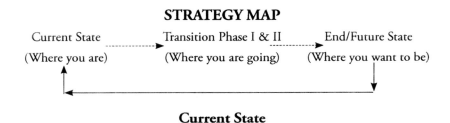

Current State

ACTION 1: Make an initial assessment of where you are. Start with what you want to do and why you want to do those things. Analyze your environment by using the brainstorming questions listed previously. Post images of your End or Future State on your social media account or print them out and place them on a corkboard somewhere in your home. Save the photo on your cell phone to constantly remind you of your vision.

ACTION 2: Identify and list your strengths, weaknesses, opportunities, and threats to achieving your goals. Leverage your strengths or core competencies. Look for ways to improve on your weaknesses, exploit opportunities, and recognize potential threats that could hinder your progress and derail your plan.

ACTION 3: Write down your core values. These are the principles and beliefs that you'll live by to help guide your daily actions in an unwavering, moral, ethical, and righteous way. For example:

Cross Bearing Charities will always demonstrate steadfast character, integrity, and honor while adhering to a standard of excellence in all that we do.

Transition Phase I

This is the most time consuming part of your plan and requires much thought to build. This is where the action occurs and where pathways to winning are identified.

ACTION 1: **Where do you see yourself one, five, or ten years from now?** Write out your vision statement. This is a statement that focuses on where you desire to be. For example, *The vision of Cross Bearing Charities is to create a poverty free world in the next ten years.*

ACTION 2. **Write out the long-term goals** that must be accomplished in order to achieve your overall vision. Focus on the "big rocks" or major things you need to accomplish. They should be S.M.A.R.T. (Specific, Measureable, Achievable, Realistic, and Time-Based).

ACTION 3. **Write out your short-term goals, objectives, priorities, and initiatives**. Use them as milestones and targets to accomplish your mission. They should be SMART (Specific, Measureable, Achievable, Realistic, and Time-Based).

ACTION 4. **Determine your priorities.** For example, God, Family, Ministry, Career, Friends.

ACTION 5. **Write out your mission statement.** This should be a comprehensive statement that explains your purpose and what you intend to achieve. For example:

The mission of Cross Bearing Charities is to provide service to people in need, to advocate for justice in social structures, and to call the entire church and other people of good will to do the same.

ACTION 6. Choose a supporting Bible verse to anchor your mission statement.

Transition Phase II

ACTION 1. Take reasonable risks by exploring three different courses of action to achieve your goals. Evaluate the pros and cons of each to find out what works best. Don't be afraid to make mistakes.

ACTION 2. Determine what resources and people you need to accomplish your goals. Ensure that you have a grading method or scorecard to evaluate your performance and track your progress.

ACTION 3. Determine your milestones, and which tasks need to be completed. Also set an estimated time for completion. Complete those tasks.

End of Future State

ACTION 1. Measure your success again and record any lessons learned. Think about how you will implement, execute, monitor, and revise your plan.

ACTION 2. Use the STOP method which simply means Stop, Think, Observe and Proceed. Stop to think about where you want to be in the long run and imagine your future state. You should imagine how things should look one to ten years from now. Make a sketch, take photos, or google a few images from the Internet that represent where you desire to be in the future.

ACTION 3. Make observations and look for opportunities to improve your strategy to determine where you can make revisions to improve your efficiency and effectiveness. Proceed with those revisions. Your future state is exactly what it says: the absolute ideal outcome you'd like to achieve. It is the destination point of your strategy map. Be flexible and adaptable to changes. Start the cycle again for each goal you intend to accomplish and don't quit.

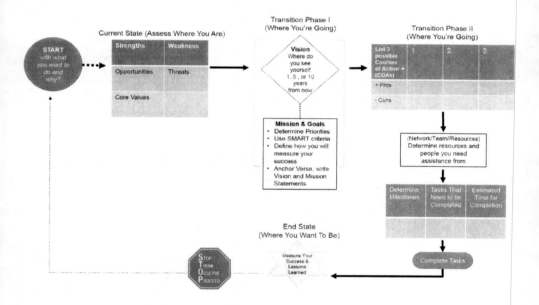

THE BEST PLAN

The best way to ensure lifelong success is to completely renew our minds through repentance. You might be asking yourself, "What does repentance have to do with thinking, planning, and succeeding big?" Let me share my rationale. I believe the greatest plan that man can experience is the plan of salvation. We spend the majority of our lives chasing dreams on earth but we fail to create a plan for what happens after we leave this earth. Our existence is comprised of our mortal life (our time here on earth), and eternal life (where we go after we die). God has had a plan for our lives since the beginning. If we follow his plan it can provide salvation, hope, comfort, and guidance now and in eternity.

The foundation of this plan can be found in Romans 10:9 that tells us, "If you declare with your mouth, 'Jesus is Lord,' and believe in your heart that God raised Him from the dead, you will be saved"(NIV). Because of our sin, we are separated from God. Romans 3:23 declares, "For all have sinned and come short of the glory of God." The Penalty for our sin is death. As found in Romans 6:23, "For the wages of sin is death, but the gift of God is eternal life in Jesus Christ our Lord." *However the* penalty for our sin was paid by Jesus Christ! God demonstrates his own love toward us, in that while we were yet sinners, Christ died for us. If we repent of our sin, then confess and trust Jesus Christ as our Lord and Savior, we will be saved from our sins. The scripture states that, "For whoever calls on the name of the Lord shall be saved" *(Romans 10:13).*

I believe it is appropriate to share the plan of salvation with you in these simple steps. Repeating the words of the Salvation Prayer alone doesn't save a person, but it is rather the power of truly believing and committing our lives to Christ as Savior and Lord that saves us. The following is merely a guideline for our sincere step of faith:

Simple Steps:

1. Acknowledge in your heart that Jesus is Lord.
2. Confess with your mouth that Jesus is Lord.

3.   Believe that Jesus died for your sins and was raised three days later.

4.   Repent of your sins and get baptized in the name of Jesus.

Prayer of Salvation

"Lord, I have sinned and I have not lived my life for you up until now. I need you in my life; I want you in my life. I sincerely believe and acknowledge the completed work of Your Son Jesus Christ in giving his life for me on the cross at Calvary, and I long to receive the forgiveness you have made freely available to me through this sacrifice. Come into my life now, Lord. Take up residence in my heart and be my king, my Lord, and my Savior. From this day forward, I will no longer be controlled by sin, or the desire to please myself, but I will follow you all the days of my life. My life is in your hands. I ask this in Jesus's precious and holy name. Amen."

If you decided to repent of your sins and receive Christ today, welcome to God's family. Now, as a way to grow closer to him, the Bible tells us to follow up on our commitment.

- Find a local church where you can worship God.
- Get baptized as instructed by Christ.
- Share your new faith in Christ with someone else.
- Spend time with God each day. It does not have to be a long period of time. Just develop the daily habit of praying to him and reading and studying his Word. Ask God to increase your faith and your understanding of the Bible. Seek out good pastors or ministry leaders to help you with this.

- Seek fellowship with other followers of Jesus. Develop a group of believing friends to answer your questions and support you.

PLAN OF SALVATION

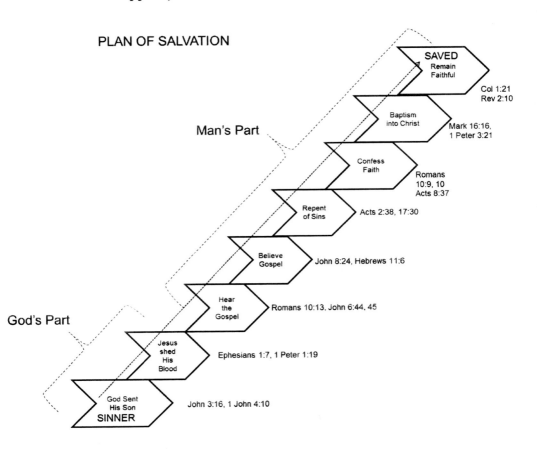

Persist Until Success Happens

Life Application Exercise

1. Using the PUSH page, take a moment to draft your own strategy. Consider the size and scope of the goals you've set and the problems that need to be solved. Use your brainstorming answers to help build greater context concerning your endeavors. Be open minded. Once you're finished, keep the ideas that are relevant to your situation and use them as the framework to build your strategic plan for success.

SMALL STEPS TOWARD BIG SUCCESS

Be flexible: In order to be successful in business or in your personal life you must be able to adapt to changing situations and environments. Things happen and sometimes even the best laid plans fail. Life is full of surprises and unanticipated challenges that can derail us if we allow them to. You must carve out room for unexpected changes, this way you'll be able to react to circumstances and redirect your efforts without having to start over. Good strategies are always built with flexible options in mind.

CHAPTER 9

HIGH ACHIEVERS BUILD DOORS

If opportunity doesn't knock, build a door.
Milton Berle

I t has been said that success occurs when preparation and opportunity meet. In a sense, society has conditioned us to prepare then *wait* for the right opportunity to present itself to us. Contrary to that belief, the doors of opportunity will not automatically swing open for you simply because you are qualified or deserving. You must remember that there is a long line of qualified people ahead of you crowding around the same doors that you want to enter. So how do you stand out in such a competitive world? The answer is quite simple—you must build your own door. People who enjoy consistent success tend to understand how to prepare, take action, and create opportunities without being opportunistic. They set themselves up for it by building doorways into the minds and hearts of the decision makers who have the power to give them an opportunity. They speak truth and provide good information that makes decisions easy and clear for the decision makers they work for. They ready their minds and use their creativity to solve tough problems that help them advance to the front of the line in any selection process.

SIX WAYS TO OPTIMIZE CAREER SUCCESS

1-Use Your Insight

Successful people gain insight about their environment and use it to their advantage. They constantly gather information, noticing things that other people do not see. They always take initiative to correct problems. For example, I once had a boss who would conduct simple tests during job interviews. He would test each candidate to see if they were paying attention to details, but more importantly whether they would take initiative to correct things that were out of order. Before each candidate entered the room, he would wad a sheet of paper into a ball and place it in the middle of the floor in front of his desk. He made sure to place it directly in the line of sight of the candidate. He would conduct his interview as normal and wait to see if the candidate would take the initiative to pick up the wad of paper and throw it in the trash bin without being told. Many candidates failed the test because they did not correct a problem that was right in front of their face. The wad of paper was a problem, and each candidate that walked past it acknowledged it as a standard that they were willing to accept. However, the best candidates corrected the problems and aced the test every time which made them more competitive and built a door to a new job opportunity.

2-Be a Natural Resource

Successful people are extremely aware, attentive, and accommodating. They know how to be a natural resource for other people. These traits help them build more doors to new opportunities. They pay attention to details and learn what kinds of things other people value and think of ways to streamline processes and make people's lives easier. They are sincere team players who know how to add value to their organizations. They understand the principle of generosity, which means that they always give more than they look to receive. They sow generously into everyone they interact with. This characteristic makes them a valuable asset to the people they work with and for. If you learn to cultivate and develop these habits, people will think of you first when they're looking to elevate, promote, or hire someone for a job.

3-Project a Positive Image

Successful people are active, visible, and project a positive image. They are keenly aware of how their public and private behavior affects their opportunities. They understand that they live in a glass house and other people are constantly observing their attitude, their demeanor, their appearance, and are forming opinions about their competence, character, and motives. For example, your demeanor, disposition, and conversational tone can determine whether or not you are selected for greater opportunities. People watch you to evaluate how you speak, respond, and interact socially with others, even when you're interacting with those people who are considered to be less important. Genuine warmth and charisma draw people to you and increase your credibility and influence. Whether people admit it or not, everyone wants to be liked and have a good reputation. Your authenticity and the way you treat people help you win influence which becomes your stamp of approval or disapproval in the court of public opinion. The truth is, if you want more opportunities there will be times you'll need earn the popular vote. However, never compromise who you are or try to be someone that you are not. In the words of William Shakespeare via Polonius, "To thine own self be true." This is a great quote but I'd like to add that in being true we must also be wise.

4- *Take Initiative*

Successful people often step up to the plate and lead—they make it happen. They've mastered the art of taking initiative and take pride in performing at the highest levels. They're internally driven toward excellence, growth, and productivity. This causes them to put forth maximum effort at all times even when it is not required. For most people, they're only using a fraction of what they have since it's not demanded in their careers. However, successful people see each day as an opportunity to improve. Over time, they become so good at what they do that it makes it hard for them to be ignored—even when they're in a follower's role. Speaking of which, there will be times when you're not necessarily the top girl or guy according to title or position. You should always learn to follow well and pay attention to what others who've gone before you have done. This will help equip and empower you to make better decisions when it's your time to lead. Never hesitate to pick up the baton when you see fit and make things happen, but make sure that you learn to support and encourage others even when they drop the baton. Just because you may have the answers or solutions to problems doesn't necessarily mean you have the right or authority to change things, especially when someone else is in charge.

5-*Provide Outstanding Assistance*

Always look for opportunities to help others while you demonstrate your finest skills in a non-threatening manner. Seek out opportunities to match your best work with the projects that people around you are doing. People may feel intimidated by your abilities, but the key is to be humble, generous, and supportive of their efforts. Go to war with your ego and win, in other words, humble yourself. Small or large, easy or tough, your goal is to provide outstanding assistance. When you perform well and are easy to work with, the news travels quickly. The word will spread and more opportunities will open up for you. People will place more value on the work you do and start to look for opportunities where they might use your higher-level abilities.

6- *Wisely Choose Your Associations*

Successful people are keenly aware of their associations. If you show me who you hang around I can immediately determine how successful you will be. You are the average of the five people you associate with most. There is an old adage that says "You can't soar with the eagles if you're always hanging out with turkeys." This means that you must evaluate your relationships. This doesn't mean that you should drop your friends, but it does mean that you should be careful about who you select to become a part of your inner circle. Your circle of influence determines how much you succeed. Colin Powell summed it up this way,

> "*The less you associate with some people, the more your life will improve. Anytime you tolerate mediocrity in others, it will increase your mediocrity. An important attribute in successful people is their impatience with negative thinking and negative acting people. As you grow, your associates will change. Some of your friends will not want you to go on. They will want you to stay where they are. Friends that don't help you climb will want you to crawl. Your friends will stretch your vision or choke your dream. Those that don't increase you will eventually decrease you.*"[30]

STRATEGIC ADVISORS

Truly successful people understand that they can't accomplish everything by themselves. They often tap into the power of networks in order to socialize their aims. Jesus had a network of twelve people and an inner network of three trusted agents that promoted his agenda and helped carry his message to the masses. He epitomized leadership and cultivated two-way relationships with his followers. He was an emotionally intelligent mentor that compelled many to leave their occupations and follow him. If you desire to be successful, you must seek out both like-minded peers and good mentors or "strategic advisors" who will provide support, direction, and help when you need it. Theses advisors have a wealth of wisdom and know how to skillfully apply their knowledge to life. You do not always need to meet a strategic advisor in person. With the advancements of technology through Facebook, Twitter, Periscope, Skype, etc., you can connect with any strategic advisor virtually 24-7 across the globe. Use social media connections to your advantage...connect with those advisors who are worth following. For some time I've watched strategic advisors, such as John Maxwell, Myles Munroe, Simon Sinek, and Jeremie Kubicek who have helped me sharpen my skillsets, but I have never met any of them personally. I read their books and studied their habits from afar to create big success in my own life. They are experts in their fields. Why not study from the best in order to become the best?

Let's take a look at John Maxwell. Few leaders have been able to distill a lifetime of leadership study into a list of guiding principles in the way that author John C. Maxwell has through his books. Maxwell is a globally recognized leadership expert who has written more than thirty books and sold more than thirteen million copies, primarily exploring the dynamic relationships that exist between leaders and followers. He is the founder of several organizations that have trained more than two million leaders worldwide, ranging from Fortune 500 companies to the Military Academy at West Point. In his book the 21 Irrefutable Laws of Leadership, (often referred as "*The 21 Laws*"), Maxwell shares timeless wisdom from his forty years of leadership successes and failures while combining them with observations from the worlds of business, politics, sports, religion, and the military. He introduced twenty-one laws or timeless leadership principles that he claims are universally true, regardless to where one may lead in society. Many of them have been helpful in assessing my personal leadership abilities as well as pinpointing target areas for growth. Throughout the book, he presents these laws as individual strategies that, when applied together, can make his leadership theories a practical reality. In my opinion, Maxwell's leadership insights were practical and many of them can easily be applied on a daily basis. For that, I'm appreciative. He does an excellent job of establishing a framework of fundamental principles to enable leadership success. John Maxwell has definitely paid it forward through his written works and lectures.

Successful people thrive on generosity and always look for ways to pay it forward. They make a commitment to serve, mentor and help others achieve their goals and dreams. No one ever reaches the highest pinnacles of success as a lone ranger—even he had a counterpart! You should always remember to reach back and offer your hand to those that are coming behind you. Be a strategic advisor to someone else. Encourage and inspire others to set and accomplish realistic goals. Help them to realize their true potential.

CAPITALIZE ON YOUR GIFT

Finally, to create doorways of opportunity you must prepare and capitalize on the gifts and talents that make you stand out. A great way to do this is by demonstrating your brilliance. Author

A.A. Milne charmingly said it this way, "Promise me you'll always remember: You're braver than you believe, stronger than you seem, and smarter than you think." Many people don't believe they are brilliant because they did not graduate from high school or college at the top of their class. But the true mark of intelligence is not always found in academic settings, on standardized tests, or in classrooms; it can show up in other ways. Never think less of yourself because you do not fit into a traditional category. In my opinion, Intelligence Quotients (IQ) tests are weak predictors for achievement, success and wealth. Brilliance can be demonstrated by the way you process information, use your talents, and display your creativity. You must take time to figure out the areas where you excel and leverage those strengths.

When legendary singer Ray Charles went blind at an early age, he could no longer depend on his vision to navigate his way through the world.[31] He began to use his hearing to determine his distance and proximity from the objects around him, and he moved around quite well on his own. He also used that same gift of hearing to play the piano and compose songs in a rich, unique, and soulful way—some would say that it was not his hands, but rather his gift of hearing that made him a musical genius. It was this brilliant gift that brought him worldwide acclaim and fame. In a similar fashion I've used my gift as a pianist to take me to places I would never have imagined. When I started developing my piano skills as a teenager I never thought I would be good enough to play gospel music with any of the legendary gospel recording artists. However, I put in a tremendous amount of time perfecting what I call the 4Ps (pray, plan, practice and perform) and it became a reality. First, I prayed to ensure that my aspirations were in alignment with God's will for my life. Once God gave me the green light, then I'd plan the best way to use my gift to glorify him. Next, I would practice and study music for several hours every day, sometimes throughout the night into the next morning. There were times that I'd forget to eat. Last, I perfected my skills so that on any given day I'd be ready to perform at a professional level. Years of training and following the 4Ps enabled me to build doors to great opportunities and big success. Over the years, I've played for gospel legends such as Vanessa Bell Armstrong, Joe Pace, Dorinda Clark Cole and other national recording artists during various concerts and events.

In order to demonstrate your brilliance, you must draw from the wellspring of knowledge and experience that you've gained throughout your life. Strive to set yourself apart in your own area of expertise. Perfect and utilize transferrable skills and build a high level of competency in your craft. In other words, become a master of your own domain and showcase your most dominant gifts to the world.

THE RIGHT OPPORTUNITIES

There are times when opportunities become so abundant that you may be unsure as to which doors you should choose. Although it can be a good problem to have, this type of situation can be just as tough as not having any opportunities at all. The key is knowing how to discern if an opportunity is a good prospect or an open door from God. You might ask, how can you tell if God is holding a door open for you? To start, you shouldn't hastily rush into every opportunity that comes along. You should pray, think objectively, and use a measured approach when you are considering which opportunities to pursue. A good rule of thumb when you're uncertain about which opportunities you should choose is to always select the ones that lead to more opportunities.

Over time, I've learned to allow God to escort me through the doors of opportunity. Doors can either give you access to the things you need inside, or keep you outside while you're being developed to handle what you're about to enter into. Through prayer, I was able to discern which doors were being pushed open by his hands. The scriptures state it this way "And I say unto you, Ask, and it shall be given you; seek, and ye shall find; knock, and it shall be opened unto you."[32] God uses different ways to direct and guide believers to and through open doors of opportunity. First, when God opens a door of opportunity, it adds meaning, purpose, and reward to our lives—without sorrow. The blessing of the Lord brings (true) riches, and he adds no sorrow to it (for it comes as a blessing from God).[33] Second, the doors he opens never contradict his Word. He will not lead you into temptation, evil, disobedience, or into a personally compromising situation. He will always lead you on a path of righteousness for his name's sake. And finally, when he opens a door, it will be accompanied by peace and confirmation through His word or from godly counsel.

You can be a successful person! Work on the behaviors that I've shared throughout this chapter. I'm sure you found some nuggets of wisdom that you can apply to multiple areas in your life. Forget about your past failures, they are not worth agonizing over. Today can be a fresh start for you. But you must modify your thinking to become more solution-oriented. Your success in life begins and ends with how effectively you access, manage, and employ your inborn gifts to build your own doors to new opportunities. No one else thinks the way you think, and no one can do things the way you do them. You may not think the world needs your ideas and gifts, but it does. You have unlimited potential and it is time for you to exploit your talents and share your gifts with the world.

We were created as a designer's original and crowned as the most highly developed life form on the planet. God designed each of us with a unique blend of intellect, gifts, and talents that He programmed within our DNA. For we are God's handiwork, created in Christ Jesus to do good works, which God prepared in advance for us to do.[34] He has given us great work to do, so we must unlock our gifts and use them effectively. When we do so, we create new doors of opportunity that help us move forward in life to positions of greater influence and success.

Persist Until Success Happens
Life Application Exercise

1. Join a good professional organization to increase your exposure to new ideas, innovations, and opportunities.

2. One thing truly successful people do is network. In the professional world, networking is a balance between corporate interests and personal relationships. It will give you the opportunity to make meaningful connections while inspiring you to attain new levels in your personal and professional development. Look for opportunities both online and in person to network. Attend social functions and mixers related to your career field.

3. Look for altruistic opportunities to use your talents to help others solve problems at your job, in your community, or at your church. Pay it forward, be generous to others by giving back on a regular basis. Local charities, soup kitchens, homeless shelters and community cleanup are good places to start.

4. Seek out good mentors and never pass up an opportunity to learn from them. It is easier to learn from those who have traveled the road that you're trying to take. They can teach you the best routes and help you identify the pathways to success.

5. Over the next year strive do to take one course or attend one seminar on the following subjects: leadership, relationships, business, finances, motivation, and spirituality.

SMALL STEPS TOWARD BIG SUCCESS

See problems as opportunities: Every plan will not be perfect, you'll never have all the information you need, and problems are a regular part of life. Whether it is money issues, misunderstandings, or time constraints—the list is endless! To achieve success, you must look at your situation from multiple angles. Successful people see every problem as a potential opportunity. When you sense a good opportunity, pray first, do your homework, seek good counsel, and trust the Holy Spirit to guide you. There will also be times when you have problems that are beyond your control and that require you to summon an outside perspective.

CHAPTER 10

GET FOCUSED

Focus brings the most important things into view.

We live in a complex and demanding world that requires us to make contributions to it daily. We are pulled in so many directions by people and issues that require our time, attention and talents. But in order to enjoy richer, fuller lives without being depleted we must make the best use of our time, have clear focus, and make our ambitions meaningful every second of the day. We must clearly identify our targets in life, take aim, and pull the trigger by instinct. This requires knowing when to use a shotgun and when to shoot with a sniper rifle. Life is all about precision and focus. In other words, we must determine the size of the goals we're pursuing and select the best instrument to use to take down our targets with the appropriate amount of firepower.

What tasks are you wasting a lot of firepower on that can be done with less energy and effort?

One of the key disciplines needed to move forward in life is the ability to focus. Focus is the result of a deliberate effort to channel your energy. Vision and focus work together in complimentary dimensions. Focus is when you narrow your vision down to specific areas and make your ambition meaningful. When you begin to focus on a single subject and excel at it, doors of opportunity will open for you. In order to do this, your mind must be clear and free of confusion or doubt about what goals it needs to focus on; it should not become easily distracted . . . good intentions, lots of determination with little focus, results in wasted effort. You must choose your targets wisely and prioritize the things that matter the most. There is a good acronym that I came across for the word *focus*:

F-Follow
O-One
C-Course
U-Until
S-Successful

Prioritizing tasks can help you achieve focus. You must decide what needs to happen at the moment, what needs to be delayed, and what can be deleted. If you do not focus on what is most important, you could inadvertently spread yourself too thin. When you spread yourself too thin, priorities become unbalanced and overloaded. You may find yourself taking on too many tasks, which may result in a lack of productivity in multiple areas. When this happens, you set yourself up for personal failure. You must manage your time in a way that helps you maximize your efficiency without losing effectiveness.

Life is full of opportunities to make focused decisions; we make hundreds of them every day. Most are easy and minor, but some require wisdom and strategy. As a teenager fresh out of high school in Pearson, Georgia, I anxiously stood at a crossroad with one foot planted in the harsh realities of rural poverty and the other foot at the threshold of uncertainty. I did not want to go to college, partially because I was unfocused, immature, academically lazy, and cheating was the easy option in high school. After I graduated from high school, I took a job as a fork lift operator at a local manufacturing plant that made cotton, paper mesh, and burlap bags. I met and worked with some great people, but I couldn't see myself doing that for the rest of my life. We should always appreciate where we come from, but we should also search for a door that opens into a better life. I also knew my parents couldn't afford to send me to any of the nearby vocational colleges. I desperately needed an exit strategy to avoid becoming another black male statistic that sold drugs or worked a minimum wage job that presented no opportunity for advancement. It was crunch time and I needed to make a smart decision to change the inevitable path my life could take.

After working all day, on many summer nights I would remove my moldy old box fan from the bedroom window of our mobile home and peer through the screen at the night wanderers passing by. Many of them roamed the streets without a sense of focus, purpose, or direction. There were other occasions, in almost perfect timing with the chirping of the crickets' chorus, when I could hear a few of our citizens singing songs as they lay drunk in a ditch under our flickering street lamp. I've always wondered why drunken people sing lively songs and then burst into tears? But I digress. I believed there had to be more than drunken serenades beyond that window screen! I needed to take a definitive step. With the swift stroke of a pen, I enlisted in the United States Air Force. It has been one of the best decisions of my life. After nearly twenty years of service, my faith, focus, and vision have been the walking sticks of my journey toward career-long fulfillment. My voyage has been great, but it hasn't always been easy.

Joining the military was an eye opener for me. During Basic Military Training our Drill Instructors would stress the importance of timeliness and paying attention to details. It was largely due to the fact that omitting minor steps could result in a major catastrophe during combat missions or in garrison. The same is true in life, the measure of success that you experience in life could come down to how much attention you've given to the details. If you've engineered a solid strategy but fail to execute of the details of the plan, you'll end up on the losing side of the contest.

In the military I developed self-discipline, stability, and structure in order to be successful in life. I was forced to do deep technical study because cheating was not an option. I began to live by the core values of "Integrity First, Service Before Self and Excellence in All We Do." I learned to prioritize my responsibilities in order to accomplish multiple tasks in a short period of time. Each day began with the trumpeted tune of Reveille and commenced with a race to get out of bed, jump into our clothes and be in formation for physical training. Our time was extremely compressed and our days were filled with many things to do. We were productively focused—both physically and intellectually. Every day I was challenged to broaden my thinking and understand the technical aspects of my job. I spent hours reading and re-reading technical manuals, instructions and professional materials over and over to learn the details of Air Force publications. The more I focused on the material, the greater my perspective widened on the subjects I studied. I gained intellectual focus in the military, and to this day it has been an invaluable commodity in my life.

When you get focused, things will come together for you and you'll start becoming more productive in multiple areas in your life. Make a promise to yourself to remain focused on your goals and your God-given assignment without letting distractions interrupt your flow. Commit to your tasks. Being successful requires an unwavering commitment toward completing your long/short term tasks, goals and projects. You should always begin tasks having the end in mind. This type of commitment requires a mind-set of understanding your milestones and striving to reach each of them on time. Do not procrastinate, because it's an enemy to achievement. Also, draw your focus away from time wasting activities such as constantly checking your smart phone, or gathering excessively near the water fountain or coffee pot at work. Learn to channel your energy toward what you can do to improve your productivity and efficiency without wasting time or losing your effectiveness.

Our overall success is highly dependent upon our productivity. Focusing helps you to identify ways to maximize your productivity. There is no shortage of good ideas, and there is always a better way to do things. Be open to alternatives such as technology, automation, and delegation to help you increase your yield in certain areas, especially those that help increase your daily output. Divide your day into thirty to forty-five minute chunks and match your tasks to those blocks of time. Some tasks will require multiple chunks of time while other require less. Look for inefficiencies in your daily routine. Whether it's starting your day early, or taking shorter lunches on certain days, blocking out uninterrupted time on your calendar for certain events, etc., strive to get the most out of every twenty-four-hour period. When you learn to manage your productivity, it will free up white space on your calendar for you to focus on the more critical issues that tend to affect your desired end state and long range goals.

BALANCING ACT

My father is the hardest working man that I have known in my life. He rises early for work and goes to bed late. Rain, shine, sleet, or snow, he is constantly on the move…building, repairing, and expanding things. I know from speaking with my aunts and uncles that he has always been that way, spending long hours in the fields and always outworking anyone around him. As a child, I never quite understood why my father worked so hard. He would always say, "Hard work never killed anybody." He also said that his father, my grandfather, taught him "You can't keep a good man down, and you sure can't prop a lazy one up." I understand the tone and tenor of their messages, but I also know that you should balance your work ethic with your family life.

You cannot always wait for the perfect timing or the best team to assemble around you. True successes require diligence on your part—just do the work! Mark Morgan Ford, a writer for the Palm Beach Letter penned an article relating to corporate work performance. In his article he highlighted several key points drawn from the studies of Saul Gellerman. He stated the following:

"According to Saul Gellerman, an expert on the subject, people at work form a bell-shaped curve when it comes to diligence and follow-through. At the bottom are the loafers and goof-offs. In the middle is the silent majority that does just enough to get by. At the top are the relative few who are motivated to achieve. When you understand the dynamics of any such group, you understand that a modest amount of hard work will put you beyond both the terminally slothful and the lump-along middle crowd."[35]

Saul Gellerman's assessment is spot on. Simply stated, sometimes all you have to do is work harder than everyone one else and you will separate yourself from the primal pack and rise to the top— exactly where you belong!

Work ethic is a societal value that runs deep around the globe. It is said the owner of the Dallas Mavericks, Mark Cuban, routinely stayed up until two in the morning and didn't take a vacation for seven years after starting his first business.[36] General Electric's CEO Jeffrey Immelt has a restless machine-like drive in pursuit of excellence. For twenty-four years he often worked one hundred hours a week.[37] He maximized and divided his time each day to deal with specific portions of his business. And Hong Kong's Li-KaShing, now age eighty-six, left school at the age of fifteen and became a factory general manager by the tender age of nineteen. He began outworking everyone as a teenager as he climbed the ladder of success to a $21 billion empire. He is now one of the richest men in Asia.[38]

I once had a boss who spent twelve to fourteen hours a day at the office. He was a highly intelligent man with a young family and was blazing a trail up the corporate ladder. He had experienced extreme success throughout every facet of his career. His dependability put him in line for early promotions on two separate occasions. After regularly working a twelve hour shift, he would leave work in the evenings and go home for dinner. After spending a few hours at home with his family, he would go back to work at midnight to catch up on administrative tasks and paperwork. He managed to keep this routine up for two years. I often wondered when he slept or spent quality time with his wife and young sons.

Many challenges will arise on your road to success, but possessing the proper work/play balance will help smooth out the ride. Being a workaholic can backfire if it is not kept in check. To successfully balance your work and family life you must appropriate your time equally to both sides without neglecting one over the other. Creating the best balance does not come naturally and requires a level of discipline to achieve, but the benefits of having a happy family and successful career are well worth the effort. If you're a person whose time is in high demand, take time to build a flexible schedule and hold calendar meetings at dinner with your family. Schedule your weekly activities as well as what you plan to do during spring and summer break or on special days. If you put marks on the calendar you are more likely not to miss important dates.

Persist Until Success Happens
Life Application Exercise

1. **Write out a to-do list of all your tasks.** Determine how long each task will take and then break them down into daily, weekly, monthly and annual tasks. Don't worry about the order, or the number of items up front.

2. **Prioritize what is urgent against what is important.** The next step is to see if you have any tasks that require urgent action. These are things that if not completed by the end of the day or in the next few hours, will have serious negative consequences (missing a tasker from your boss; missed project or release deadlines, etc.). Check to see if there are any competing high-priority dependencies that are in the chain of events that rely on you finishing up a certain task now.

3. **Assess the relative significance or biggest payoff of each task.** Next, look at your important work and identify what is most significant to your household, career, ministry, business or organization. As a general practice, you want to recognize exactly which types of tasks have top priority over the others. For example, focus on: your boss's projects/deadline before helping out a peer or subordinate. Another way to assess value is to look at how many people are impacted by your work. In general, the more people involved or impacted, the higher the stakes.

4. **Order your tasks by the estimated effort required to complete them.** If you have tasks that seem to tie for priority standing, check their estimates, and start on whichever one you think will take the most time energy and effort to complete.

Productivity experts suggest the tactic of starting the lengthier task first. But, if you feel like you can't focus on your longer projects before you finish up the shorter task, then do it first. I follow the two-minute rule which says that if you can do a task in under two minutes, you should do it immediately. It helps ward off procrastination and keeps the minor issues from piling up.

5. **Flexibility is the key**. Even with the best laid plans and schedules, things will inevitably change and interruptions will occur. When you acknowledge these possibilities, you'll be ready to respond accordingly. Know that your priorities will change, and often when you least expect them to; however stay focused on the tasks you're committed to completing.

SMALL STEPS TOWARD BIG SUCCESS

Strike a good balance: Dream chasing can devour much of our time and resources. In order to be successful you must be disciplined when it comes to balancing your life. Everyone gets the same twenty-four-hour period to manage. It's easy to allow the daily grind to take control of your life, leaving you void of joy in the things that you want to accomplish. You must take time for daily prayer, reading, meditation, exercise, and healthy eating. Evaluate which tasks are value added and which tasks are profit driven. Decide what can be deleted, delegated, or delayed from your task list. Last, plan your free time and hold calendar meetings every week with your family and key staff at your job.

CHAPTER 11

PLAY TO WIN

*Make each quarter count, and play every second
in the game of life as if it was your last.*

American culture places tremendous value on winning and being successful because those things typically correspond with our life plans. When we reach certain milestones in those plans such as completing school, landing a great job, or launching a new business from home, they bring us fulfillment through the visible progress we've made. At times you may be tempted to try to accelerate your success because you feel pressured to keep pace with what others have done during certain seasons in their lives. In the end, only you can determine the pace of your journey, and it's only your opinion of it that matters. Don't compete with others, compete against yourself and win. In other words, set personal development goals and strive to be the best version of you that you can be.

Keep in mind that life is a marathon event that tests your endurance, mental strength, and courage to stay the course. Ultimately, you succeed by settling into a strategically set pace to cross the finish line without quitting. Throughout your race there will be hills, valleys, and long stretches when you're separated from the pack. At times you might experience bottlenecks where you're closed in by the herd, but you must continue to run your race. At other times you may stumble and fall, but get back up and look for the aid stations. Use them as often as you need them, but whatever you do—don't quit. Keep pushing!

TRUE CHAMPION

To win at anything worthwhile, you must be persistent and have a strategy. I recognized early on that I needed to have the heart of a lion and be as tough as nails. As I stepped onto the court I thought about all the hard lessons I had learned during my backyard scraps with my older brother and sisters. The time had finally come to put my athletic skills to the test. There was less than a minute and twenty-three seconds left on the game clock in a real nail-biter. I slowly limped to the free throw line as the deafening throb of my heartbeat in my throat drowned out the roar of the coliseum crowd. My palms sweated and my ankle ballooned with pain from a sprain I'd suffered the night before during the semifinal game against Paideia High School.

Our team had come so far that year, with a record of twenty-three wins and nine losses. We had accomplished the unthinkable by pulling off stunning upsets on the road against both Treutlen and Terrell County High Schools. From a little country town littered with abject poverty, our motley crew of underdogs had finally made it to the big dance at the State Finals! To call it a Cinderella journey would be an understatement. We were the most unlikely team to win.

Most of our team had grown up shooting hoops together as kids in the neighborhood, or just across the railroad tracks from each other. In bare feet (or busted up Nikes with mismatched shoelaces), we played ball from sun up to sun down, as if it were our full time job. Whether we played in the trampled dirt patches in the sawmill quarters, or the slick unfinished hardwood of our dilapidated neighborhood gym, basketball was the common thread that knitted all of us together.

My freshman through junior years in high school had whizzed by in a blur and this was my last chance to make a mark in the record books. For me and three other seniors, it would be our final time stepping onto the court together. We had a monster season, but our journey into our final season was definitely not without hardships. Just two seasons before, our squad had tasted the sweet nectar of victory and in the same bite we swallowed the bitterness of tragedy through the loss of a teammate.

As I stood behind the free throw line preparing to take my shot, my mind flashed back to a day that I will never forget. On October 25, 1992 one of our teammates had been fatally shot and killed by a co-worker at his job. This violent event took a heavy emotional toll on our team. He was a star athlete who dominated the court with perfect shooting form, speed, and God-given agility. He poured his heart and soul into the game and was truly destined to play at the collegiate level. He was just seventeen years old and expecting his first child (born four weeks after this tragic event). We carried his memorial in our hearts for several seasons, but somehow throughout the years, we transformed our grief into pure motivation to win. Because of his death, I learned four valuable life lessons: (1) make each day count, (2) take shots when you have them, (3) give maximum effort in everything you do, (4) and play every second of the game of life as if it were your last.

The game clock stood still and the distractions coming from behind the basket from the opposing fans were unnerving. I was exhausted but I squared up on the hoop, took two dribbles, a deep breath, and released the ball. I visualized the ball going through the hoop and hearing the snap as it dropped from the bottom of the net. I thought about how good it would feel to seal the deal and bring home the championship trophy. We were on the cusp of being the first and only team in our school's history to win a state champion-ship in boys' basketball. Then it happened...

We all sensed it—we were in the zone. We had combined our strengths to compensate for our weaknesses. We'd adapted to the sit-uation by relying on our speed, our defense, and the court awareness we had developed playing together in the neighborhood. Without saying a word to each other, we felt the pounding rhythm and roar of our talents combine to shift the momentum of the game. From that point on, our chemistry was locked, every rebound, every play, every bucket was nothing but net! The seconds rapidly ticked off the clock in our favor... the crowd echoed five, four, three, two, *one*! The horn sounded. We had pulled it off and written history. We had become the Georgia High School Association (Class A) Boy's State Basketball champions!

EIGHT PATHWAYS TO WINNING

As I've looked back on that time, I've come to realize that the closer we got to our goal, the tougher the opponents were. Each team we faced was bigger, faster, and stronger than the team before. There was nothing we could do about that. The courts, baskets, and rules couldn't be adjusted to give us an advantage. But what we lacked in physicality, we made up for through teamwork and our will to win. Sometimes in life, the closer you get to your goals, the greater the opposition and resistance becomes. After that game, I learned several lessons that have served me well as I push forward in life.

First, you must prepare yourself to win. Some say that prac-tice makes perfect, but I believe that perfect practice makes perfect. You must always push yourself toward perfect results during your moments of preparation if you want to reach new heights. You must build the right habits, discipline, and behaviors in order to master certain skills. Coach Bobby Knight said, "The key is not the will to win... everybody has that. It is the will to prepare to win that is important."

Second, you must push yourself in short productive bursts. When you're setting out to achieve goals, it's best to complete a lot of short term goals first. Seeing a trail of small accomplishments will invigorate you. It will give you the extra mental energy to push when you're completely exhausted or burned out. Lastly, it will also help you build your tolerance and train your mind for completing bigger and more time consuming goals.

Third, you must always push beyond your limits. Always convince yourself to take one more step. Never stop or give up at the same place you did before. When you're nauseous and out of breath and feel that you can't move another inch, dig deep and push as hard as you can to go a bit farther.

Fourth, you should push yourself to play with pain. During the championship game my ankle had swollen to nearly double its size and I could barely walk. But I knew how important it was for me to play in that game. You must learn to play the game when you're hurt, happy, sad, confused, frustrated etc. Champions never quit, they always find a way to keep going forward. It is said that Michael Jordan played a game with flu-like symptoms and scored thirty-eight points. Playing in pain maybe the toughest challenge of them all as we try to avoid it when possible, but as the old saying goes—"no pain, no gain."

Fifth, you should push yourself to play by the rules. I've learned that you shouldn't focus on manipulating the rules of the game or use unprincipled means in order to win. You've earned your spot on the playing field and can achieve victory in an honorable way—with integrity.

Sixth, you must push with all of your strength and will. Your will is perhaps one of the most powerful forces on earth. It helps drive us through tough situations. There are numerous accounts of people who were on their death bed, or in a dangerous situation who tapped into unusual spiritual strength in order to survive.

Seventh, you must push under control. All thrust and no vector gets you nowhere in a hurry. Having self-control is fundamental to success. You must channel your energy in the right direction and be in control of your efforts. Also, you must learn how to control your emotions. It enables you to think more clearly, perform on higher levels and see the pathway to winning when it is not so obvious.

Finally, you should push to win the home court advantage. Always be aware of your environment and know who and where you're playing. Learn to exploit early advantages and capitalize on that success. Constantly look to gain the home court advantage so that you can control the environment and play at your best. In order to get the home court advantage you must have a better record than your opponent. For example, if you are in a job situation with a manipulative co-worker, never go head to head with them on their court. Look for ways to support them in their endeavors (except when it is immoral, unethical, or unsafe). When you support your co-worker (even a bad one) you gain the home court advantage by taking the moral high road. Each time you do this, you achieve a personal victory in your life by doing the right thing and ultimately improve your record.

It has been over twenty years since that game and I still get excited when I think about it. Occasionally when I dust off my championship ring, I remember the feel of the momentum swing during that final game. As I reminisce, it rekindles the intoxicating feelings and emotions that connect me to that moment. Through the years, I've come to realize that this emotionally sweet victory added value to my existence. It continues to inspire me to work hard and develop winning habits to be victorious in the most important game of all—the game of life.

FIND YOUR WHY

Highly successful people tend to have a "why" in life. In other words, they have vision, passion, and righteous motives behind their actions. Their "why" originates from the core of their being (their spirit and will) and it fuels their inborn drive. When people identify their "why" it sparks their passion and puts them in a mode of relentless pursuit to raise their personal performance bar. During our state championship game, I knew the reasons "why" I wanted to win and capitalized on them in order to help push our team to victory. I did not play for the sake of securing my own legacy—I played to inspire hope in my hometown.

Take a moment to consider who you seek to inspire through the things that you accomplish in life.

Success becomes more meaningful when we expand beyond our own interests and consider the desires of those we lead and serve in our communities and our world. We must see the enduring impacts our actions have on the lives of others. Success is more satisfying when you have people to share it with. Since that day, I've come to understand that God has an assignment for anyone who is willing to be used by him—especially underdogs! Today, I live by the cardinal confession that Christ gives me strength and I can do all things through him. With the deepest sense of humility, I realize that my success originates through him and empowers me to thrive as a servant leader. It motivates me to do my best for my family and others who are encouraged by the wisdom that I share from my broad experiences and professional successes. Bearing the right motives in mind, I absolutely believe that you can and *will* do much more.

BE A GAME CHANGER

Every so often great people come along with big ideas that make such a tremendous impact in our world that they completely shatter the status quo and cause a paradigm shift. In the business world they are often referred to as "game changers."[39] King Solomon was one of the earliest examples of someone who could be considered a game changer. In King Solomon's case, his extreme wisdom and success completely redefined monarchial prestige. He was highly sought after for his insight and regarded as a prolific writer, poet, and botanist. His skills in architecture and management changed Israel into a thriving showplace in the Middle East.[40] His material wealth, influence, and wisdom remain unmatched to this day. As a result, he has been regarded as one of the most successful men in history. He was outrageously blessed, but he also experienced his fair share of personal failures. Despite his failures, have you ever wondered what made King Solomon so successful in comparison to other kings?

Social media outlets make it appear that billionaire millennials like Facebook co-founder Mark Zuckerberg are overnight successes in the social media game—adding to the exception and not the rule.[41] Game changers like Zuckerberg develop their sense of direction early on and are extremely strategic when they make their moves. It's the behind the scenes studies they conduct to strengthen their core competencies that make them masters of their universe. Without perspective it's easy to believe that anyone can stumble onto becoming an overnight success story. The truth is that Zuckerberg experienced his fair share of failures; but he continued to work hard and tenaciously strategized his way to the top of the social media game after he had dropped out of Harvard. To this day he continues to be action oriented with a relentless sense of urgency for getting things done as he crushes his competition.

Often we see other media moguls like Oprah Winfrey (CEO of Oprah Winfrey Network and Harpo Productions) who have dominated their fields without having the benefit of seeing them fight through their lifelong processes to be successful. Oprah triumphed over considerable hardships throughout her childhood to become an iconic African American billionaire. [42] She was able to leap high enough over her obstacles to shatter glass ceilings in the media industry.

Now please don't equate the accumulation of wealth as the essence of all success, because in some cases it is simply a by-product of it. Have you ever thought about what drove these people to the pinnacle of success? The common thread that exists between them all is quite simple—game changers are "problem solvers." You see, as long as humans inhabit the earth, there will always be problems. People who are exceptionally good at solving problems always gain a distinct advantage over their competition in terms of respect and influence. The bigger the problem they can solve, the greater their span of influence becomes. Let's quickly examine Solomon's case.

In the third chapter of I Kings, Solomon wisely resolves a dispute between two mothers about who the rightful parent of a newborn baby is. The mechanism (game) he uses to determine which mother is the true parent begins when he recommends the baby be divided in half and each mother be given one half. Obviously the true mother can't bear the agony of seeing her baby sliced in half, so she screams, "No! Let the other woman have the baby instead." Her loving plea to save the baby obviously reveals who the rightful mother is. In another instance, King Solomon takes on a construction project that his father, King David, was unable to complete. He solves a divine problem by erecting an opulent earthly house for the living God. God endorses his efforts and Solomon's reputation for successful problem solving flourishes.

Mark Zuckerberg identified the problem of friends not being able to connect socially through the Internet, so he created an online networking platform where it could be done. In Oprah's case, she recognized the need for a more confessional venue within the daytime talk show genre. She used her compelling personality to revolutionize her show, providing an intimate setting that appealed to a massive national audience.

In each case, these game changers stepped back and allowed their creativity and innovation to take center stage. Perhaps it's time for you to tap into the reservoirs of your own problem solving abilities and start building a strategy that will help you become a game changer in your field of expertise. Find problems that you care about and start solving them. Use your critical thinking skills to examine problems at home, on your job, or in your community. Ask God for wisdom and strategies and He'll give you the answers you need. Realize that you won't be able to fix all of the world's problems by yourself, but you'll be able to contribute and make a tremendous difference in your sphere of influence.

THREE BIG WAYS TO BECOME A GAME CHANGER

1. *Be business minded.* Game changers have a knack for starting and completing new projects and doing business. They conduct research and ensure they have good data before they make decisions. They cross their "I's" and dot their "T's" especially when it involves brokering deals, creating products, and getting things done. They are intently focused on the goals they set.

2. *Incubate your ideas.* Game changers water the seeds of daydreaming in a quiet and methodical manner. They put themselves

in the right environment, around the right people in order for their ideas to be nourished with positivity. They understand how important it is to plan and innovate. Even if an idea you have leads to a successful project or venture, it usually takes time to refine a concept before it makes any sense, however they remain patient with the planning process.

3. *Grind daily.* Game changers understand that anything worth having will not come easy. They are relentless when dealing with giant obstacles. They have an aggressive hustle for solving problems. They refuse to collapse under the burden of their challenges. They take calculated risks knowing that the bigger the risks are, the greater the reward.

Persist Until Success Happens
Life Application Exercise

Take a moment to study the three ways to become a game changer

1. This week share one of your ideas with someone who is very trustworthy. Get their honest feedback and opinions.

2. Focus and get one overdue project done over the next two weeks. Whether at home or work, if your projects are ultimately shelved, postponed, or constantly changed, you could end up getting frustrated and never complete anything.

3. Choose one problem that you're currently facing and explore different ways to solve it. Don't be afraid to ask for outside help or ideas.

SMALL STEPS TOWARD BIG SUCCESS

Unity of effort: It's been said that team work makes the dream work. As you grow and become a person of influence or game changer, the majority of your success will be determined by the strength of your team. You must master the art of working well with others to get the greatest yield from your efforts. Use discernment when choosing trusted agents or teammates, and make it a point to inspire and develop their talents. Take the time to ask for your team members' opinions and listen carefully to each person's viewpoint. This promotes mutual respect and trust. Praise your team in public and reserve your criticism for closed door meetings. Compliment your team for jobs well done; it will go a long way.

CHAPTER 12

FINDING YOUR NICHE

One of the greatest moments in your life occurs when you figure out what you were created to do.

YOU ARE WIRED WITH PURPOSE

Have you ever wondered, "What is my purpose?" or "How can I awaken my passion to successfully move forward in life?" These are common questions that many of us have wrestled with at one time or another. It is what I call, "the search for significance." Humans are wired with an instinctive curiosity to find out what we were created to do. All too often, people devote their lives to pursuing goals that were not defined by them in order to feel a sense of self-worth and accomplishment. They struggle to find their life flow and spend their existence fulfilling other people's dreams. This makes it difficult for them to realize their true purpose and to thrive in their own element. They'd rather retreat behind the curtains of someone else's ideas and opinions than take center stage in doing what really makes them feel alive and happy. However when you find you purpose it liberates you from the burden that prevents you from being the best you can be.

For many of us there is a gap between the life we are leading and the life that we feel we are destined to live. Too many of us spend the majority of our lives doing jobs or activities that we may not necessarily believe in or feel truly motivated by. We are simply existing rather than thriving and this can become a frustrating ordeal. It can eventually become a major source of stress. The late Dr. Myles Munroe said, "The greatest tragedy in life is not death, but a life without a purpose." This is a weighty statement indeed! The toughest part for many of us is first recognizing our purpose and then rising to its call. We discover our purpose when the highest and best expressions of our God-given gifts contribute to a cause that is greater than ourselves. If we search carefully, the core of it stems from a divine need to utilize our talents in concert with God's will for our lives. When we operate in alignment with God's will, He begins to animate our purpose by making it come alive! Once we recognize and understand our purpose, we can channel our efforts to drive our dreams forward with unlimited success. We can rid ourselves of counterproductive behaviors and self-defeating mindsets and begin to thrive in life.

PINPOINTING YOUR PASSION

Our search for true purpose should cause us to do some self-reflection. It should cause us to honestly survey our abilities to find out where our passion or sweet spots are in life. What do you have a true knack for? What fascinates you? What is on your mind when you go to sleep or when you wake up? What gives you that overwhelming rush of adrenaline and goose bumps when you know that you've *nailed* it? Maybe it's being a makeup artist, writing short stories, landscaping, or teaching people to play the piano. Finding our sweet spot in life comes from a much deeper place than we can imagine. It resides deep within our souls. When we find it, it beautifully compliments who we are and fills us with complete joy and passion.

The things you are passionate about should be energizing and nourishing. They should not constantly drain or frustrate you. Your purpose should be something you connect with emotionally, not just intellectually. It should be grand and inspiring, something worth building your life around. Your passion becomes heightened over time as a result of being successful in your efforts. It is cultivated through concentrated work, as you vector your natural talents toward things that reward you the most.

Imagine that you started a very challenging tennis class and found it to be easy. You realized that you were excelling at a much faster rate than others. You began to experience an excitement that caused you to push yourself harder in every session. Each time you grew hungrier to improve and build on your success to get better results. Now, you just can't go a day without attending a training session and you invite others to join you. This is an example of developing a passion for something that you have a knack for. If you haven't found your passion yet, don't leave it to fate. Never stop looking for it.

If you are still unsure about your purpose or passion, the questions on the PUSH Page will help put you on the path to finding them.

Persist Until Success Happens
Life Application Exercise

Write down your answers to the following questions.

1. What do you do with your time that is vitally important? How much time did you spend doing things that were personally meaningful?

2. What are you good at that gives you true joy?

3. What adds meaning to your life?

4. How can you use your gifts and talents to make a difference in the world?

5. What risks are you not willing to take even though your gut screams "Go for it!"?

6. What do people value most about you?

7. What do you think about constantly?

8. Determine your why. Why are you doing the things that you are doing? Are you really doing what you were created to do?

9. What are your unique gifts and talents?

10. What were you doing when you were at your best?

11. Who must you fearlessly become in order to achieve your goals?

SMALL STEPS TOWARD BIG SUCCESS

Go for it: One of the first steps to experience success is to know what you want and cultivate a strong desire to go for it. Once you have discovered what you desire, develop a clear picture in your mind that you have achieved it. Hold this mental picture in order to create an indelible imprint on your subconscious mind. Use this image to fuel your drive.

CHAPTER 13

EMPOWERED FOR SUCCESS

Your future will only produce as much as you've sown into it today. Invest in yourself!

Empowerment is a wildly popular term that resonates across many motivational and spiritual arenas. It takes on different meanings depending on the person and context. I define personal empowerment as the by-product of being equipped to release your potential. Fellow theologian Dr. Charles Stanley sums up empowerment as "the divine energy that God is willing to express in and through us and the divine authority needed to carry out the work that God has called us to do." I fully concur with the proposition that the ultimate level of the human experience extends into the spiritual realm. Just as we feed our physical bodies with food, we must also feed our spirits and minds through faith. Many people find empowerment and motivation through their faith and I happen to be one of them.

I have always desired to be a game changer, someone with high influence capital, and a convincing knack for inspiring people. I strongly sensed I was destined to be a leader, but I didn't clearly know which vehicle would take me there. When I was younger, I envisioned sitting at the head of a highly polished mahogany boardroom table with a team of executives who possessed the power, ability, and influence to shape the world. Today I'm deeply humbled to say that I'm living out my vision every day of the week. I've traveled across the globe and lived in foreign countries, led hundreds of people, overseen millions of dollars in budgets and advised foreign leaders and government officials on goal setting and completing strategic objectives. My faith in God has been essential to my professional success and has empowered me to make critical decisions without hesitation.

In essence, empowered people turn their freedom of choice into action. They act on their internal values with courage. This in turn enables them to better influence the course of their lives, the lives of others, and the decisions that affect them. Personal empowerment is not a static thing you can do or experience once in your life, but it is a constantly evolving process of enablement and development. Let's put things in context and bring this word a little closer to our everyday situations.

Most people dream of being successful in life, but many of them do not achieve success because they view their prospects through the lens of past failures. They do not feel empowered or possess the courage to change their situations. In other words, they anticipate their future will result in more moments of letdown based on their history and current environment. Sometimes we cling to previous assumptions rather than recognize the changes in the environment in front of us. We have a natural tendency to expect that every day will be the same and never plan for what could happen next or open our eyes to what is happening now.

A number of years ago, I had the opportunity to advise a foreign leader of a war torn country about how to develop solid strategies to rebuild his country's future. I was sent to do a tough job. My eyes burned as I patiently sat in the middle of a smoke-filled room, occasionally sipping on the Chai Tea that was prepared by my Arab hosts. As time ticked away, I gently reeled in the opportunity to steer our lengthy conversation. One of my toughest challenges during our negotiations was convincing him to embrace his potential for creating the change that was needed in his country.

After lighting another cigarette and slowly drawing it closer to his body, I recognized that my host was stuck behind a wall of resistance due to cultural impasses and prevailing ideologies. I began to understand that in order for me to successfully negotiate with him I would have to meet his resistance with compassion. I knew that he had the necessary insight to create change, but he did not feel empowered to take action to bring it about. He doubted his power and ability to take the wheel and drive the proposed changes through with success. As a result, he missed a key opportunity to help steer security and stability in his own country for generations to come. From that day forward I understood why empowerment was so important.

At some point, we are all thrown into situations that prompt us to make pivotal life choices to bring about transformation. Despite our recognition that changes have to be made, for some people, the actual act of implementing change is not all that easy. Sometimes it takes true courage to overcome our own lack of confidence and the pressure from others in order to bring about positive change. There will be times when you must take unpopular stances and be willing to face the criticism that follows after you've challenged the status quo.

Through wisdom, perseverance and self-discipline, you can use empowerment to your advantage. First, we become empowered by identifying that we have choices versus thinking or believing that we have no options. This strengthens our base for decision-making. Secondly, you must know your own power, be able to access it, and use it appropriately. If you look closely, you'll recognize that you have more power than you think. Finally, you should prepare for and maximize any opportunity that you're given to expand your influence. In other words, widen your social networks so that you can build credibility among larger groups. When you broaden your influence base, you'll be able to achieve more.

INVEST IN YOURSELF

Empowerment enriches the soil that allows your talents to sprout. It provides the proper base that is needed to thrive and perform at peak levels. To be your best, begin investing time, money, and effort into empowering yourself. Your future will only produce as much as you've sown into it today! Your success is directly linked to investments that you make in yourself. Warren Buffet once said, "Invest in as much of yourself as you can, you are your own biggest asset by far." The amount of commitment and effort you put toward investing in yourself can significantly impact the quality of your life now and in days to come.

People who have been successful and productive in our world place a priority on investing in both personal and professional growth through their commitment to self-improvement. One way to do this is by constantly developing your own talents and skills. Our Creator has designed each one of us with a distinctive blend of powerful talents and gifts that make us unique. The scriptures read, "I will praise thee; for I am fearfully and wonderfully made."[43] In other words, you are a highly developed creation loaded with hidden potential that must be unearthed. It is our responsibility to cultivate and develop the gifts we were given. We should seek out knowledge about how to improve upon them daily.

Our empowerment rises as we build our personal and professional knowledge. Knowledge, skills, and experience are important assets that we acquire over a lifetime and they can take many forms.

Knowledge tells us what to do in order to reach the next level. Most people gain knowledge through advanced academic degrees, training, and certifications. However, your quest to expand your knowledge and skills doesn't have to be limited to formal brick and mortar institutions. We live in a data driven society that offers information pertaining to just about every subject imaginable. With today's resources and technological advancements, there are numerous other informal avenues by which you can gain knowledge and information such as workshops, conferences, and webinars.

Never pass up an opportunity to acquire knowledge. Finish high school and go to college—it's never too late! I absolutely hated school when I was younger, not because I didn't like to learn, but because I was immature. When I joined the military, a good friend of mine challenged me to take a college course. I refused to take his challenge because I didn't want to fail and lose face with my friends. Plus, I had been told by a few people that I would never go to college, and I believed it. I had been out of high school for several years, and I thought it would be too difficult to start up again. But my friend never gave up and told me he would even take a class with me. After much nagging, and of course this was the final straw, I took him up on his offer. I took an English class because I was fairly decent at writing and suspected I could probably squeak by in the course with a passing grade. So I enrolled. Then I actually began to enjoy the class. I learned how to write college level essays and began to understand the framework for structuring my thoughts in a logical manner. After weeks of writing I felt that I was improving, but couldn't determine how much I had improved. I worked hard and did my best, but I was nervous about turning in my final paper to my professor. I went through so many versions that I literally ran out of time, so I had to take a hard copy to his house after class. For weeks I dreaded seeing my grade for the course and knew that if I didn't maintain a certain grade point average I would have to repay all the money the military had given me to take the course. After weeks of praying and waiting I finally received my grade. Much to my surprise I passed the course—with an A.

That single grade boosted my confidence and inspired me to continue my education. It sparked a fire in my belly and I developed a passion to do whatever it took to earn a college degree. Early in my military career I worked on airplanes five days a week and every third or fourth weekend for twelve hours a day in the blistering Texas sun. After a hard day's work, I would leave my job with greasy hands and dirty fingernails and sit in a class in oil-soaked clothing for several hours. I also attended summer school and any additional courses they offered. I used my lunch breaks and often took leave to take classes. I cut out extracurricular activities so that I could do homework. I stayed up many nights until the next day, completing assignments, sometimes holding my young daughter on my lap. If I had to deploy, I'd study on the airplane during transit. I took out loans to cover the cost of my books when I ran short on money. I sold some of my things to scrape up money because I didn't want to go into debt. I also worked a second job at a retail clothing store in the mall to help fund my education. Today I have two associate degrees, bachelors, two master's degrees, and a doctorate. I always graduated with top honors each time. Someone may be wondering, with all those things going on when did I find time to sleep—my answer is…I didn't. I learned that if a person wants something bad enough, they will figure out how to get it done without excuses or sleep. Maybe college isn't for you, but that isn't a good excuse not to continue learning.

Take time to read books, articles, or papers on subjects that relate to helping you develop your talent. Do research and stay current with the latest trends. Leverage opportunities to listen to the experts on different subjects. Cross-pollinate the info that you acquire. Learn about other aspects of the field that you desire to be successful in. Study widely to ensure you're exposed to different perspectives. Use that cross-functional knowledge and perspective and weave applicable portions into your own strategy for success.

Another way to encourage empowerment is by exploring your creative side. Learn to think outside the box. When you explore the creative side of your mind, you open up a passageway to put your ideas and natural talents to work. This outlet enables your inborn abilities to surface. Learning new things and keeping your mind active, even in simple ways, helps grow and maintain your mental ability. You can also stimulate your creativity by exploring the world around you. When was the last time you attended a performance or went to an exhibit? When was the last time you took on a new project or craft such as drawing, painting, woodworking, sculpting, embroidery, knitting, or photography? Have you stretched yourself to learn a new language or challenged yourself in a unique way?

Tapping into the creative side of our minds stimulates personal growth and development by helping us view and analyze issues from different perspectives. It helps us become more effective problem solvers. When you become a problem solver, you raise your individual value and expand your sphere of influence. There is not a single major corporation or business in operation today that doesn't want problem solvers on its team.

To be successful, we must take active roles in controlling the course of our lives. Please don't struggle with this idea. I understand that you can't control everything and by no means am I suggesting that you should try—it's absolutely impossible! What I am suggesting is that you use your power to take action, add to what you're given, and become more than just a product of your environment. Take a more assertive role; wield your influence to impact the people around you and in your world in a more meaningful way.

Instead of relying on outside influences for motivation, find it within yourself. Personal empowerment begins with making a quality decision, and that decision is all yours. Take control of your own future and use the pressure that you're under to fuel your drive to succeed. When you take responsibility for your achievements, development, and ambition, there is no limit to what you can accomplish. You're the captain of your ship. Set sail and nothing will stop you!

Persist Until Success Happens
Life Application Exercise

Take a moment to incorporate the Empowerment Strategies listed below into your life strategy:

1. Pray and engage in positive confessions daily and convince yourself that you want to be successful.

2. Take control of the wheel and drive forward!

3. Network and surround yourself with other successful people to expand your influence.

4. Invest in yourself by gaining knowledge.

5. Be a problem solver.

6. Remember your why.

7. Remain positive.

SMALL STEPS TOWARD BIG SUCCESS

Develop a thirst for knowledge: Successful people never stop learning and they constantly search for opportunities to grow, improve, and sharpen their skills. Conduct a personal assessment and draft a list of areas you want to improve. Then search for ways to get formal and informal training to improve your existing capabilities. This will help you develop the whole person concept. At least twice a year, strive to attend a conference. Most companies have lunch-and-learn sessions; take them whenever they are available. Seek out mentors that have traveled the path and learn what they know. Enroll in online courses or webinars and subscribe to applicable professional blogs to expand your knowledge and optimize your performance. If you own a business, survey your customers to find out what they need and value most.

CHAPTER 14

THE POWER OF CHARACTER

*Character is the essence of who we are. It's a key
component to succeeding with dignity.*

It would be unreasonable for me to speak about success without adding the word "character" to the conversation. Character is defined as a "complex of mental and ethical traits", that those traits, or qualities, are "distinctive to an individual" and that they are "built into an individual's life."[44] Throughout history and in every pocket of society, we have seen highly successful people fall apart ethically and morally due to the lack of good character. You may be wondering how this happens. It's quite simple. At some point it each of their lives, they allowed their integrity to become a casualty of their ambitions. The old adage "you are what you do" is true. In other words, they became so intoxicated during their drive toward success that it impaired their judgment and set them on a collision course to failure and embarrassment.

Everything that we accomplish in this world occurs as a result of the individual choices we make and the qualities that make up our character. Successful people possess certain character strengths that put them in a position of upward mobility. It is the foundation of their achievements. Most importantly, the quality of their character determines whether they experience sustained success in their personal and professional lives. It is the core of who they are and is wrapped in their actions, beliefs, and thoughts. Character is developed over time. It is a self-imposed discipline that keeps our lives in check. It should control our lifestyles in an honorable way, acting as an alarm in our conscious that goes off when it is violated. It also helps us to maintain an image of power and correctness.

Most people link character to personality traits, and they are in fact closely related, but they are not one and the same. Personality consists of your inborn traits, but character refers to learned behaviors that we can develop and shape over time. In other words, character is an unwavering commitment to a set of prescribed moral standards and values.

Let's examine some of the traits that help us more clearly define what character truly is. Let's start with humility. Successful people are humbly aware of their vulnerabilities. Serving in different leadership capacities I've learned that being humble, credible, and approachable will help you win the endearment of your people. Being humble refers to the way a person genuinely regards themselves among others. It's having a clear perspective of where we stand in relation to others and thinking less about ourselves. Keep in mind that no matter how good looking, smart, powerful or successful you are, no one likes a self-absorbed arrogant person. We should never look down on anyone because of their status or stage in life. I think of it as killing self-pride in order to serve others, which is a true mark of maturity.

When you are humble, it creates a level of comfort between you and other people that can open more dialogue between you. In a social context, it enables others to relate to you and open up and share things that could be beneficial to your success. It can cause people to seek you out for sound advice because, in their eyes, you have become a personable trusted agent. Yes, being humble does all of these things!

The next character trait we'll take a look at is courage. It has been the mark of all great leaders, past and present. Courage requires us to overcome our fears and stand bravely in the face of adversity. Having courage does not mean that one is absent of fear, but rather speaks to how one acts to overcome fear. Courage demonstrates to the world the kind of person you are under pressure. It takes moral courage to own your mistakes and admit when you're wrong. It takes courage to tell the truth especially when lying will get you off the hook. Being courageous gets tougher as the stakes grow higher.

Being courageous makes me think of the movie the *Wizard of Oz* and the Cowardly Lion. In the movie, the lion believes that his fear makes him inadequate, especially because lions are supposed to be the kings of the jungle. The lion doesn't realize that as he accompanies others in often treacherous situations, his instinctive (and courageous) reactions often help protect the group.

What you must keep in mind at all times is that occasionally fear will be a factor in the game of life. On our road to success, we'll all be challenged to call on our courage to protect ourselves and those in our group. I can assure you that when it's needed the most, you will find you have more courage than you think.

Another trait that helps us build character is having an attitude of gratitude. Counting our blessings helps us realize that we truly don't deserve all of the things that God has blessed us with. It is easy to get complacent and start embracing a sense of entitlement, especially when we live a life of privilege. Being grateful helps us appreciate the fact that we're more fortunate than we deserve.

Compassion is another character trait that successful people often possess. Compassionate people always look for opportunities to show their concern for other people's suffering. It's extending a caring hand to those who are in need. It's doing good deeds unto others as you would have them to do unto you.

Another character trait is being truthful. This means that you are honest in your words and actions. If you tell a person that you're going to do something, you should always do it. If you can't do certain things, then do not make promises that you do not intend to deliver on. Other people will trust you when they know that your word is your bond. It strengthens your credibility. There is a wonderful sense of joy that comes as result of knowing that you're trustworthy and honest in your dealings with other people and that others know and count on that. You should always tell the truth (in a loving manner of course) and be a person of integrity at all times, even when no one is expecting you to be. Having this quality shows the sheer strength of your character.

ESTABLISH YOUR ETHICAL CODES

Ethical codes are the morals, values, and principles we live by that guide our thoughts, behavior and deeds. They help us make the distinction between what is right and wrong and apply that understanding to make decisions. They are our core values coated with the necessary integrity to influence our conduct. Ethical codes are the personal rules we live by that anchor our success. They can be drawn from our religious or spiritual beliefs.

Persist Until Success Happens
Life Application Exercise

1. If you don't have a personal code of ethics take the time to develop one and start living by it. Begin by writing down words such as integrity, excellence, honor, and courage and then define what those words mean to you. You can also expand your code to apply to your family and business. Once you are finished, create a document or a screen saver on your phone or computer that you can look at every day to serve as a reminder of what you believe in.

SMALL STEPS TOWARD BIG SUCCESS

Maintain your integrity: To be successful, you must be conscious of your actions. Always strive to do the right thing—even when no one is looking. This helps you condition your actions. Your word is your bond and your reputation matters. So be above board, just, fair, and ethical in your dealings with everyone you meet.

NOTES

CHAPTER 1

1. James 2:14-18 (King James Version)
2. https://training.tonyrobbins.com/the-6-human-needs-why-we-do-what-we-do/
3. Psalms 46:1 (NIV)
4. Philippians 4:8 (New Living Translation)

CHAPTER 4

5. Ephesians 4:22-24 (New Living Translation)
6. http://www.khouse.org/articles/1996/277/ Be Ye Transformed What Is Mind Renewal & Why Is It So Important? by *Nancy Missler*

CHAPTER 3

7. Matthew 6:31-34 (New King James Version)
8. http://www.cbsnews.com/pictures/celebs-who-went-from-failures-to-success-stories/8/
9. http://www.learninginfo.org/einstein-learning-disability.htm
10. http://abcnews.go.com/Technology/steve-jobs-fire-company/story?id=14683754

CHAPTER 5

11. Romans 15:13 (KJV)
12. http://www.etymonline.com/index.php?term=optimism

13. Lecture on Emotional Intelligence by Dr. Patricia Maggard, Air Command and Staff College

CHAPTER 6
14. Habakkuk 2:2 (Message Bible)
15. http://www.tuskegee.edu/about_us/legacy_of_fame/tuskegee_airmen/tuskegee_airmen_facts.aspx

CHAPTER 7
16. Taken from: 12 Questions to Ask Before You Marry by Clayton and Charie King. Published by Harvest House Publishers, Eugene,http://www.relevantmagazine.com/life/whole-life/features/26675-signs-you-need-to-grow-up#y541O8HMZkrOsTWX.99
17. Jack Fallow, Friday April 11, 2003, The Guardian, Elliott Jaques Analysing Business, the Army and Our Midlife Crises. http://www.theguardian.com/education/2003/apr/11/highereducation.uk1
18. http://www.rasmussenreports.com/public_content/lifestyle/general_lifestyle/february_2013/86_believe_individuals_make_their_own_success
19. 2 Corinthians 5:7 (King James Version)
20. Twenty-One Success Secrets of Self-Made Millionaires by Brian Tracy

CHAPTER 8
21. http://www.merriam-webster.com/dictionary/success
22. Proverbs 16:3 (New Living Translation)
23. Proverbs 19:21 (New International Version)
24. Is Strategic Planning Biblical? Looking at leaders from scripture. Mark Marshall, http://www.christianitytoday.com/le/2007/july-online-only/le-031112a.html?start=2

25. 1 Samuel 17:36

26. The Origin of Strategy by: Rich Horwath. http://www.strategyskills.com/Articles_Samples/origin_strategy.pdf

27. http://www.ccsnh.edu/sites/default/files/content/documents/CCSNH%20MLC%20HABITS%20OF%20MIND%20COSTA-KALLICK%20DESCRIPTION%201-8-10.pdf

28. https://en.wikipedia.org/wiki/SMART_criteria

29. Psalm 37:23

CHAPTER 9

30. https://www.goodreads.com/author/quotes/138507.Colin_Powell

31. http://www.encyclopedia.com/topic/Ray_Charles.aspx

32. Luke 11:9 (King James Version)

33. Proverbs 10:22 (Amplified Bible)

34. Ephesians 2:10 (New International Version)

CHAPTER 10

35. http://www.earlytorise.com/the-best-way-to-surpass-your-peers-and-rise-to-the-top-of-any-business/

36. http://www.businessinsider.com/hardest-working-successful-people-2013-10#dallas-mavericks-owner-mark-cuban-didnt-take-a-vacation-for-seven-years-while-starting-his-first-business-1

37. http://www.businessinsider.com/hardest-working-successful-people-2013-10#ge-ceo-jeffrey-immelt-spent-24-years-putting-in-100-hour-weeks-15

38. http://www.businessinsider.com/hardest-working-successful-people-2013-10#hong-kong-business-magnate-li-ka-shing-became-a-factory-general-manager-by-age-19-6

CHAPTER 11

39. http://www.investopedia.com/terms/g/game-changer.asp
40. I Kings (King James Version)
41. http://www.biography.com/people/mark-zuckerberg-507402#time-at-harvard
42. http://www.biography.com/people/oprah-winfrey-9534419#the-oprah-winfrey-network

CHAPTER 13

43. Psalm 139:14 (King James Version)

CHAPTER 14

44. http://www.merriam-webster.com/dictionary/character

CPSIA information can be obtained
at www.ICGtesting.com
Printed in the USA
FFOW02n1347041017
40691FF